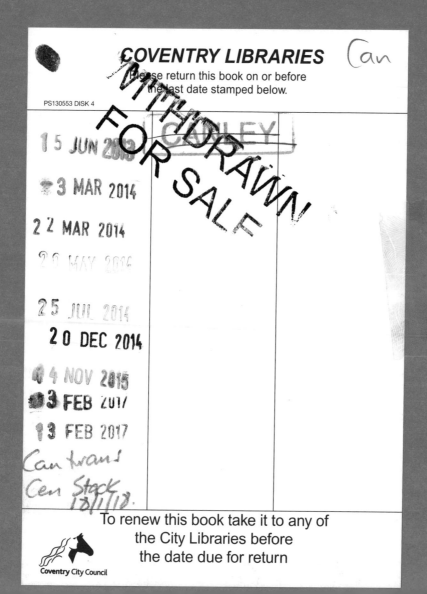

Foreword by Aled Jones

What Do You Believe?

A DORLING KINDERSLEY BOOK

LONDON, NEW YORK, MUNICH,
MELBOURNE, and DELHI

Senior Editor Fleur Star
Senior Art Editor Hedi Hunter
Editors Holly Beaumont, Lorrie Mack, Lee Wilson
Designers Karen Hood, Mary Sandberg

Picture researcher Rob Nunn
Production editor Sean Daly
Production controller Claire Pearson
Jacket designer Natalie Godwin
Publishing manager Bridget Giles
Art director Martin Wilson
Creative director Jane Bull
Publisher Mary Ling

Consultant Dr Gavin Hyman

First published in Great Britain in 2011 by
Dorling Kindersley Limited
80 Strand, London WC2R 0RL

A CIP catalogue record for this book
is available from the British Library.

ISBN: 978-1-40536-285-6

Colour reproduction by MDP, UK
Printed and bound in China by Toppan

Discover more at
www.dk.com

Hinduism
Bahai
Confucianism
Judaism
Islam
Christianity
Buddhism
Sikhism

It's not fair!
What have
I done to
deserve this?

"Have you ever wondered why we're here? Or what happens after we die? Or whether there's a God, and if there is, what's He (or She or It) for? Or maybe you're just curious about why some people wear turbans, or eat fish on Friday, or what words like "kosher" and "halal" mean. All these things are connected with religion, and for millions and millions of people, religion is incredibly important – it's a major force in our world.

This book examines all the main faiths – what they're about and why – and looks at how faith affects who people are, and how they live. It also asks many questions about religion itself, and explores subjects ranging from native beliefs to modern pick-and-mix spirituality and the ongoing arguments between religion and science. These chapters will not only provide you with lots of new and fascinating facts, they will also encourage you to ask questions, inspire you to find out more, and help you to answer the most important question of all: what do you believe?"

Aled Jones

ALED JONES

CONTENTS

IN THE *beginning...*

As long as there have been people on Earth, *religion has been around* to help them figure out how life works.

But what were the *first* religions? How did they *start*? And *where* did all this happen?

Early civilizations worshipped **things in nature**, from the Sun and stars to cats and cows. They believed in gods who controlled harvests, and war, and hunting, and made **simple bargains** with them ("If I kill my goat, you'll protect my crops").

Over hundreds of years, the major faiths grew and spread. Today, millions of people follow them, but some form their own beliefs, and others have given up on religion all together...

WHY believe?

For as long as there have been people, there has been the **need** for them to **believe** in something (or Someone). *A belief system* is a way of

Believe in what?

This book explores different *religions and philosophies* that accept a **higher purpose beyond this life**.

Some are *monotheistic* (*they believe in one God*), some are *polytheistic* (*they believe in many gods*), and some are *atheistic* (*they don't believe in God*).

What *is* a religion?

... and the main beliefs and practices of *world religions*.

Discover the *seven dimensions* that describe a religion...

YOU *don't have to* **believe** to *read* this book.

understanding the world. It can give *answers* to life's really big questions, such as, *why are we here?* And *what happens after we die?* Religion, faith, or philosophy can provide some people with a sense of **comfort** and **community** – yet for others, it does **nothing at all**.

Why do *people* believe?

Some people are *born into* a particular religion, while others **choose** to accept a faith.

Religion can provide answers that give people a sense of purpose – but it can also raise a lot more questions!

But I *don't* believe!

You could call *atheism* *(belief that there is no God)* and *agnosticism* *(uncertainty about God's existence)* belief systems.

Atheists generally *don't believe* in a higher purpose and meaning beyond this life.

But you can find out what *motivates people* to think and act as they do. Through **UNDERSTANDING**, we can have **TOLERANCE** and **RESPECT**.

In EARLIER *times*

People in the ancient world used art and artefacts to express their religious beliefs. Their carvings, paintings, and amazing feats of engineering give us a glimpse into their world of worship and ritual.

LIFE AS WE KNOW IT... THE FIRST MODERN HUMANS APPEARED AROUND 200,000 YEARS AGO.

STONEHENGE

This ancient stone circle in southern England is dotted with prehistoric burial mounds and ceremonial avenues. Nobody really knows why it was built or what the ancient Britons used it for, but historians suggest that it could have been part of an astronomical calendar or a site of pagan worship or sacrifice. Modern pagans still visit Stonehenge to celebrate the summer and winter solstices.

The 60 stones were rearranged in around 1500 BCE.

15,000 BCE   **3100 BCE**   **3000 BCE**

CAVE ART

In caves across France and Spain, ancient paintings reveal a world in which wild cattle, deer, and horses roamed alongside lions, panthers, and rhinos. Some experts think that these animal drawings are evidence of special rituals.

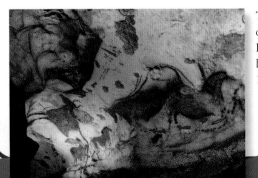

The Lascaux cave in France dates back to about 15,000 BCE.

TEMPLE TOWERS

Sumer (now modern-day Iraq) was one of the first great civilizations. Priests ruled both religious and political life and were seen as representatives of gods on Earth. Each city-state had its own god and the Sumerians built giant structures called ziggurats in their honour.

Enki, the Sumerian god of water.

A GALLERY OF GODS

Many of the gods and goddesses of the Egyptian world represented natural forces, such as the Sun, wind, and rain. They were often represented as animals (for example, the Sun god was a hawk, and the harvest goddess a cobra), as seen in paintings and carvings discovered in ancient temples and tombs. Pharaohs were also regarded as gods, and there is even mention in Egyptian texts of "The God" – an unnamed universal power.

Horus, god of the king, sky, and war.

IT'S A GOD'S LIFE!

2500 BCE   1500 BCE   447 BCE

I'LL PROTECT YOU.

ANCESTOR WORSHIP

The Chinese Shang Dynasty kings communicated with the spirits of their ancestors through oracle bones. When a decision was needed, priests would scratch a question into a shell or bone and then make cracks in the surface using a heated metal rod. The pattern of cracks were "read" as an answer from the ancestor spirits.

WHAT A GODDESS!

The ancient Greeks worshipped many gods and goddesses, such as Athena, the protector of Athens. The Greeks were also influenced by philosophers such as Plato and Socrates, who mused on the gods, the meaning of life, and the existence of an afterlife.

Athena, goddess of crafts, wisdom, and military strategy.

11

On to *India*

India has a rich and ancient religious tradition. Hinduism developed here more than 5,000 years ago. Over time, other belief systems took shape and attracted many followers: Jainism, Buddhism, and Sikhism.

SACRED SCRIPTURE

The *Vedas* are ancient sacred Hindu writings containing divine revelations. They were passed on by word-of-mouth for hundreds of years before being divided into four parts by the great sage Vyasa Krishna Dwaipayana. The four *Vedas* contain guidance on rituals, sacrifice, and prayer to the gods, who live in a Universe divided into the Earth, the atmosphere, and the sky.

Vyasa is believed to be the literary incarnation of the god Krishna.

2300s BCE   1500s BCE

INDUS VALLEY CIVILIZATION

The Indus Valley civilization, from which Hinduism came, probably existed between c. 2300–2000 BCE in what is now present-day Pakistan. The civilization is so ancient, only artefacts remain to give hints of religious ritual and worship. Archaeological finds include altar-like structures suggesting animal sacrifice, the remains of a large bathing pool (possibly used for ritual washing), and terracotta figures that may represent deities.

This ancient seal comes from a city called Mohenjo-daro – "Mound of the Dead".

This statue may represent a fertility god.

This statue of Mahavira is in a Jain temple in Rajasthan, India.

Brihadisvara Temple, Thanjavur, India

FREEING THE SOUL

Buddhism and Jainism rejected the authority of the *Vedas* and the emphasis on sacrifice and ritual. They believed that the most important goal in life was developing spiritual knowledge of the self and the Universe.

THE GUPTA EMPIRE

This was the Golden Age of India: a time when culture and religion flourished. *Puja* (devotional worship) in temples became popular and different strands of Hinduism developed.

500s BCE

300s CE

1500s CE

BUDDHISM BEGINS

When Prince Siddhartha Gautama left his palace in northern India, he was shocked by the poverty in the world. No one could explain it to him so he sat under the Bodhi tree and meditated... and found enlightenment. He became known as the Buddha (the Enlightened One), and spent the rest of his life teaching others how to achieve the same freedom and contentment.

Guru Gobind Singh, the 10th Guru, 1666–1708 CE

SIKHISM

Sikhism was founded by a succession of ten Gurus, or holy men. The first was Guru Nanak, whose belief that there is only one god formed the basis of the Sikh religion. Other gurus added elements to the religion over the next 240 years.

13

Meanwhile, in the Middle East...

The major monotheistic world faiths have their origins in the Middle East: Judaism, Christianity, and Islam. Zoroastrianism is from the same region, but centres on a duality – the battle between good and evil.

IT'S OFFICIAL!

Zoroastrianism began in north-east Persia (now Iran) when the priest Zarathustra (Zoroaster) had divine visions. He saw the world as a battle between Ahura Mazda (the force for good) and Angra Mainyu (the force for evil). It went against the tradition of animal sacrifices and worship of nature gods, but a local king adopted the religion for his small kingdom. In time Zoroastrianism spread throughout Persia, a major world empire.

Zarathustra lived in a time of idol worship.

MIDDLE EAST
THIS WAY

2000 BCE   1200 BCE   1000 BCE

God told Abraham that his descendants would be as many as the stars in the sky.

FATHER ABRAHAM

Jewish scripture states that Abraham was chosen by God to be father of a great nation. Abraham, his son Isaac, and his grandson Jacob are regarded by Jews as the fathers of Judaism. Abraham also had a child called Ishmael. Muslims see Ishmael as the father of Arab nations. Judaism, Christianity, and Islam are sometimes called the Abrahamic religions.

IT'S *LAW*!

Moses was the leader of the Hebrews (Jews) – and the prophet to whom God revealed His Torah, which is the basis of Jewish law. The Torah says that God made a covenant (agreement) with Moses, promising to lead the Hebrews to the promised land of Canaan (now Israel).

Paul's missionary
journeys

CONVERSION *IN A FLASH*

The growth of Christianity was largely the result of the preachings of Paul – a man who once persecuted Christians! Paul received a blinding vision from God in an encounter near Damascus, Syria, which led to his conversion to Christianity. Between 46–68 CE, he visited churches around the Mediterranean. He believed that everyone had access to God, not just a chosen few. Many of his teachings are written as letters and some are documented in the Bible.

PROPHET MUHAMMAD

Muslims consider Muhammad to be the last of a line of prophets that includes Abraham, Moses, and Jesus. For 23 years, Muhammad received divine revelations via the angel Gabriel (Jibreel). He established Islam, which then spread through the Middle East.

The Qur'an is
the revelation
Muhammad heard.

C. 30 CE   46 CE   610 CE   632 CE

Ali became the fourth
caliph in 656 CE.

JESUS, SON OF GOD

At the heart of Christianity is Jesus, believed to be the Son of God. The Bible reports that Jesus from Galilee (in Israel) preached about God's kingdom for three years, saying he spoke with God's authority. He angered the Jewish authorities and Romans and was eventually crucified. His followers witnessed his resurrection and proclaimed him to be the Messiah (saviour) of all nations.

CALIPHS RULE, OK?

After Muhammad's death in 632, Abu Bakr became the caliph (leader) of Islam. The Arab nation grew during this time, but after the death of the fourth caliph (Ali – Muhammad's son-in-law), the Muslim community split. Some saw the descendents of Ali as the only legitimate successors of Muhammad. They divided from the Muslim majority (later known as Sunni) and became known as Shia Muslims.

Abu Bakr was caliph
from 632 to 634.

To ENLIGHTENMENT *and beyond*

The Middle Ages onwards saw major changes in across Europe: divisions within Christianity and Judaism, the rise of scientific authority, and the questioning of religious truths and values.

THE BIG SPLIT

Christianity was the official religion of the Roman Empire from the end of the 4th century. However, after the empire collapsed c. 476, a rift grew between the eastern Greek-speaking churches and the western Latin-speaking churches. In 1054, due to disagreements on the nature of the Trinity and the authority of the Pope, the Christian church split into the Roman Catholic Church (west) and the Eastern Orthodox Church (east).

Roman Catholicism

Eastern Orthodoxy

WEST **EAST**

1054 1517 1530s

WE PROTEST!

In his *95 Theses*, published in 1517, German priest Martin Luther protested against the Church and the power it wielded. He was excommunicated in 1521, but his views – which became known as Protestantism – continued to gain popularity throughout Europe.

REFORMING EUROPE

The growth of Protestant churches in Europe in the 1520s–1530s became known as the Reformation. Martin Luther, Calvin, and Zwingli spearheaded Church reform in parts of Europe, severing ties with the Pope. In 1534, England's King Henry VIII made himself head of the church. This led to the growth of Protestantism in England.

Protestants stressed the importance of the Bible's authority.

THE AGE OF ENLIGHTENMENT

An increase in exploration and scientific discoveries from the 1600s onwards enlarged people's view of the world and ushered in the Age of Enlightenment of the 1700s. Increasingly, intellectuals applied scientific methods to discuss religious truths and values. They argued that reason freed people from religious superstition and intolerance, allowing them to think for themselves. Although religious truths weren't necessarily rejected, the church ceased to be the sole authority on truth.

> "THE FIRST PRECEPT WAS NEVER TO ACCEPT A THING AS TRUE UNTIL I KNEW IT AS SUCH WITHOUT A SINGLE DOUBT."

The ideas of French philosopher René Descartes (1596–1650) were influential during the Age of Enlightenment.

BAHAI

The 1800s wasn't only about science. In 1844 in Iran, a prophet called The Bab declared a new prophet would follow Muhammad (a claim rejected by Islam). In 1863, Baha'u'llah founded Bahai.

The Bahai symbol

1700s	1800s	1844	1859

HOW UNORTHODOX!

The first Jewish Reform synagogue was established in Seesen, Germany, in 1810. The Reform movement arose a couple of decades earlier, when many German Jews were abandoning their religion in the modern world. Reform Judaism got rid of core Jewish practices (such as keeping kosher) in the hope that it would stop people leaving the faith altogether. Many practices were later re-adopted in a less strict form.

Seesen

A RADICAL IDEA

In 1859, Charles Darwin published *On the Origin of the Species*, his scientific theory of the evolution (gradual development) of animals. Conflict arose between the Church and its explanation of the Universe and believers in evolution – although many, including Darwin, saw no problem in believing in both God and evolution.

17

Introducing the main religions (also known as belief systems, faiths, or worldviews) in the world today...

What do they *teach*?
What do they expect from their *followers*?
And what makes them *different* to the others?

When you read about different religions, you'll see them in the context of your own way of life. (This is generally how people understand each other.) But bear in mind that **what you understand as an outsider might not be how a follower of the religion sees it.**

It is also important to remember that each believer has their own level of observance (so some will do more than others and some will do less than others).

STUDYING *RELIGION*

In the past, religion was usually studied by religious people, who asked questions according to their own beliefs. About 50 years ago, writer and professor Ninian Smart pioneered *secular* religious studies – studying religion like you study geography. But some people wonder if there can be a truly objective view of religion, since our understanding is always coloured by our own ideas.

What is FAITH?

To have faith is to have great trust in something or someone. Religious faith could be trust or confidence in God (as in Christianity), or in one view of reality (as in Buddhism). Some people think faith must be based on evidence, but others believe evidence applies only to this world, not to God or higher truths.

Is *belief* important?

For some, belief is central to religion. Belief in God, for example, might be the basis for a religious life. For others, belief is in the background – what's important is practising their religion, and living a certain way of life.

WHAT *is* a

Religion is a way of *answering* life's **big** questions:

Why are we **here?**

THE SEVEN DIMENSIONS

Defining what a religion is can be very difficult. Not all religions feature God or gods; some insist their followers wear certain clothes or avoid certain food, but others have no such rules. So what do they have in common? Ninian Smart found seven *"dimensions"* that appear in all religions to a greater or lesser degree:

● Practice and ritual

Any action that is associated with religion. For example, festivals, a wedding service, and prayer are rituals, while practices may include avoiding certain food.

● Experience and emotion

Religious experience can range from a small, internal guiding voice to seeing God through visions, revelations, or miracles.

● Narrative and myth

Myths are historical tales about God or gods. Every religion has stories, both written and oral (spoken), that relate its history and provide examples of how to live.

RELIGION?

What happens *after* we die?

A religion is often described by the kind of "theism" it is. The word *theos* is Greek for God. **From this root we get:**

Monotheism — belief in one God, such as in Judaism (from *monos*, "single, alone"). His name is written with a capital G.

Polytheism — belief in many gods, such as in Hinduism (from *polys*, "much"). They are written with a small g.

Pantheism — literally means "all is God": the belief that He is all of the Universe and is found in nature on Earth (from *pan*, "all").

Panentheism — this means that "all is in God": the belief that the physical Universe is a part of God, but He is also more than that (from *pan*, "all" and *en*, "in").

Agnosticism — the belief that there isn't enough evidence to decide if there is a God or not (from *a-*,"not", and *gnosis*, "knowledge"). Scientist and philosopher Thomas Huxley, who coined the word, claimed that the question of whether God exists or not is unanswerable, and so should remain unanswered.

Atheism — belief that there is no God or gods, such as in humanism (from *a-*, meaning "not").

Some religions – such as Buddhism – have no concept of theism at all (which is why there is no "God" dimension in Smart's description of religion).

Doctrines or philosophies

Closely related to and often developed from the narratives, doctrines are the official rules and teachings of a religion.

Ethics and laws

The morals and laws that teach how a person should live and behave. Like the teachings, some laws may change over time.

Society and institutions

This is the physical impact of a religion on a person's life. It includes the organization of a religion, for example through the church and church leaders.

Material things

All objects that relate to a religion, from temples and other buildings to art, icons, and items used in rituals. Places are part of this too, including holy sites such as Jerusalem.

Religion ROUND-UP

RELIGION/ WORLDVIEW	HOW MANY GODS?	WHAT HAPPENS AFTER DEATH?	MAIN PRACTICES	MAIN SCRIPTURES
BUDDHISM	None (but some Mahayanas believe in lesser gods)	Rebirth (reincarnation) or enlightenment	Living by the Five Precepts and the Noble Eightfold Path. Meditation, mandalas, and mantras help people achieve enlightenment	*Tipitaka* (*sutras, vinaya, abhidharma*)
CHRISTIANITY	One (in the form of the Trinity – Father, Son, and Holy Spirit)	Heaven or hell	Prayer, church attendance, Eucharist (also called Holy Communion)	Bible (Old Testament and New Testament)
HINDUISM	Many (which are all manifestations of one supreme power, Brahman)	Rebirth (reincarnation) or *moksha* (spiritual liberation)	Living according to their role in life (*dharma*); worship of a god (*puja*); meditation and yoga	*Vedas* (including *Upanishads*), *Bhagavad Gita*
ISLAM	One (*Allah*)	Paradise (*Jannah*) or hell (*Jahannam*)	Living by the Five Pillars, including prayer five times a day; eating halal food; no alcohol	Qur'an
JUDAISM	One	The World to Come (*Olam ha-Ba*) – heaven (*Gan Eden*) and hell (*Gehinnom*)	Following the commandments in the Torah, including eating kosher food and praying three times a day, and observing the Shabbat	*Tanakh* (Hebrew Bible, including the Torah)
SIKHISM	One (*Ik Onkar*)	Rebirth (reincarnation) until merging with the Supreme Soul	The Five K's (symbols worn by members of the *Khalsa*); importance of doing good deeds and keeping God in mind at all times	*Sri Guru Granth Sahib, Dasam Granth*

There are thought to be HUNDREDS, if not *thousands,* of **different** religions in the world. This chart introduces the **six main** world religions.

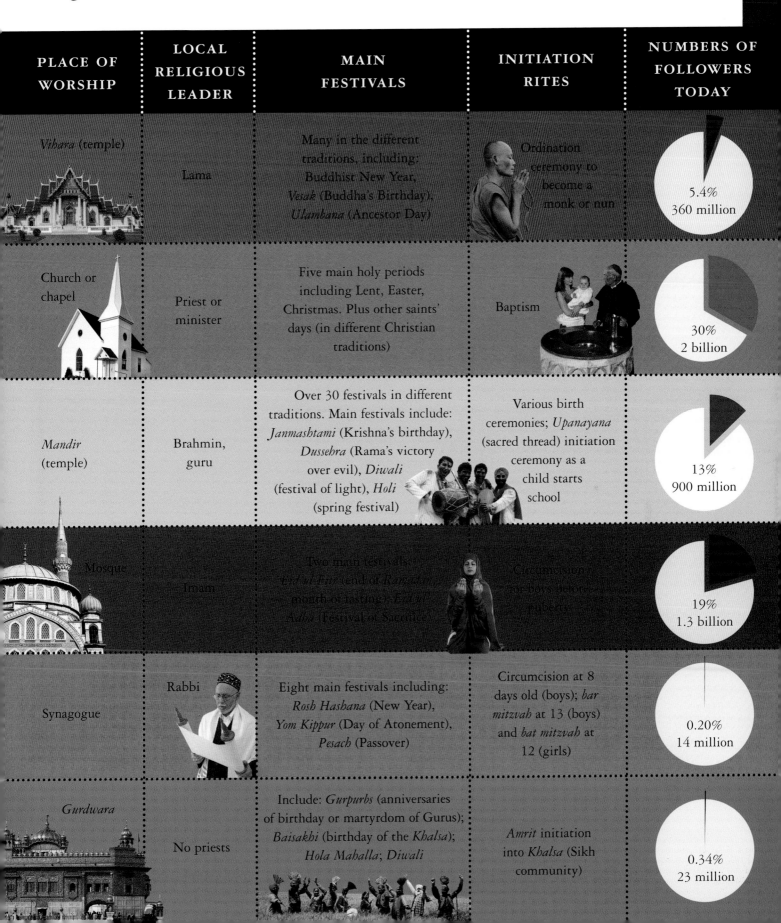

PLACE OF WORSHIP	LOCAL RELIGIOUS LEADER	MAIN FESTIVALS	INITIATION RITES	NUMBERS OF FOLLOWERS TODAY
Vihara (temple)	Lama	Many in the different traditions, including: Buddhist New Year, *Vesak* (Buddha's Birthday), *Ulambana* (Ancestor Day)	Ordination ceremony to become a monk or nun	5.4% 360 million
Church or chapel	Priest or minister	Five main holy periods including Lent, Easter, Christmas. Plus other saints' days (in different Christian traditions)	Baptism	30% 2 billion
Mandir (temple)	Brahmin, guru	Over 30 festivals in different traditions. Main festivals include: *Janmashtami* (Krishna's birthday), *Dussehra* (Rama's victory over evil), *Diwali* (festival of light), *Holi* (spring festival)	Various birth ceremonies; *Upanayana* (sacred thread) initiation ceremony as a child starts school	13% 900 million
Mosque	Imam	Two main festivals: *Eid-ul-Fitr* (end of Ramadan, month of fasting), *Eid-ul-Adha* (Festival of Sacrifice)	Circumcision for boys before puberty	19% 1.3 billion
Synagogue	Rabbi	Eight main festivals including: *Rosh Hashana* (New Year), *Yom Kippur* (Day of Atonement), *Pesach* (Passover)	Circumcision at 8 days old (boys); *bar mitzvah* at 13 (boys) and *bat mitzvah* at 12 (girls)	0.20% 14 million
Gurdwara	No priests	Include: *Gurpurbs* (anniversaries of birthday or martyrdom of Gurus); *Baisakhi* (birthday of the *Khalsa*); *Hola Mahalla*; *Diwali*	*Amrit* initiation into *Khalsa* (Sikh community)	0.34% 23 million

ISLAM
Date: 622 CE
Place: Saudi Arabia
Founder: Muhammad
Main messages: There is one God (Allah). • God revealed His final message – the Qur'an – to the prophet Muhammad. • People must submit to God's will to gain entry to paradise after death.

JUDAISM
Date: 20th century BCE
Place: Israel
Founders: Abraham, Moses
Main messages: There is one God. • Life in the World to Come is achieved through following God's commandments as set out in the Torah. • Emphasis is more on action than belief.

JAINISM
Date: c. 550 CE
Place: Eastern India
Founder: Mahavira
Main messages: There are many gods. • The soul is eternal and will be reincarnated (reborn). • Escaping reincarnation is achieved through avoiding bad *karma*, especially by not causing harm to any living being.

JEHOVAH'S WITNESSES
Date: 1879
Place: Pennsylvania, USA
Founder: Charles Taze Russell
Main messages: Based in Christianity. • Jesus is God's first creation (not the Son of God). • There will be an Armageddon (conflict) at the end of time, after which Witnesses will achieve salvation.

CHURCH OF JESUS CHRIST OF LATTER-DAY SAINTS (MORMONS)
Date: 1830
Place: New York State, USA
Founder: Joseph Smith Jr
Main messages: Based in Christianity, but the Trinity are three separate beings. • Salvation comes through following the teachings in the Gospels (books in the New Testament).

WHEN, where, who, *what*?

This map shows where some of today's most popular religions started. Some share *common roots*, with neighbouring religions influencing one another, or later faiths EXPANDING on teachings of earlier ones. Most have spread **worldwide**, but some (such as Shinto) are practised only *locally*.

North America

South America

RASTAFARIANISM
Date: 1920s
Place: Jamaica
Founder: Marcus Garvey
Main messages: God (called Jah) appeared on Earth as Jesus and as Haile Selassie I (King of Ethiopia 1930–1974). • Africa is heaven on Earth.

INTERNATIONAL SOCIETY FOR KRISHNA CONSCIOUSNESS (ISKCON)
Date: 1966
Place: New York, NY, USA
Founder: Bhaktivedanta Swami Prabhupada
Main messages: Based in Hinduism, but Krishna is the Supreme Being. • One must be pure to escape reincarnation. Chanting helps achieve this purity.

CHRISTIANITY
Date: c. 30 CE
Place: Israel
Founder: Jesus Christ
Main messages: There is one God in the form of the Trinity (Father, Son, and Holy Spirit). • Jesus is the Son of God who appeared on Earth. • Jesus was crucified and resurrected in order to save people from sin.

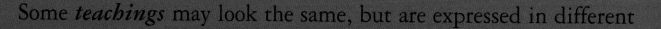

Some *teachings* may look the same, but are expressed in different

BAHAI
Date: 1863
Founder: Baha'u'llah
Place: Tehran, Iran
Main messages: There is one God who reveals His message through different prophets and religions. • All people in the world are part of the same community and should be treated equally and fairly.

BUDDHISM

Date: 520 CE
Place: Northeastern India
Founder: Siddhartha Gautama, the Buddha
Main messages: When you die, you will be reincarnated. • Your actions (*karma*) in this life determine your next life. • The aim of life is to escape reincarnation through enlightenment.

SIKHISM
Date: c. 1500 CE
Place: Punjab, India
Founder: Guru Nanak
Main messages: Life is about giving up temptation and living in accordance with God's will. • People are reincarnated (reborn) until they come into line with God's will.

SHINTO

Date: prehistoric
Founder: None – it's a collection of different Japanese traditions
Main messages: People must live in harmony with the world. • There are countless *kami* (gods and ancestor spirits), who can help people achieve harmony. • The *kami* must be properly looked after and worshipped.

Europe

Asia

Africa

Australia

TAOISM

Date: 2nd century BCE
Place: China
Founders: Laozi and Zhuangzi
Main messages: Tao ("the Way") is the essential principle of the Universe. It is found in everything. • The purpose of life is to achieve harmony by keeping yin and yang in balance.

ZOROASTRIANISM
Date: c. 1200 BCE
Place: Persia (modern-day Iran)
Founder: Zarathustra (Zoroaster)
Main messages: There is one God (Ahura Mazda) but also an evil spirit (Angra Mainyu) who is almost as powerful. • Life is a choice between good and evil. People must choose good to unite heaven and Earth.

HINDUISM

Date: prehistoric
Founder: None – it's a collection of different Indian traditions
Main messages: There are many gods who are all incarnations of the Supreme Reality (Brahman). • People are trapped in a cycle of rebirth based on the actions (*karma*) of their current life. • Escaping rebirth (*nirvana*) means uniting with Brahman.

CONFUCIANISM
Date: 6th–5th centuries BCE
Place: China
Founder: Confucius
Main messages: *Taiji* is the unknowable force that controls the Universe. • The Universe is made up of two fundamental principles: yin and yang. • The balance between them affects the harmony of life.

ways *in practice* (and in most religions, it's **practice** that counts).

What is JUDAISM

PRINCIPLES OF FAITH

Judaism doesn't have an official creed (statement of belief), but it does have the Thirteen Principles of Faith. Each starts **"I believe with perfect faith…"**

1 … that God is the Creator and Ruler of all things. He alone has made, does make, and will make all things.

2 … that God is One. There is no unity that is in any way like His. He alone is our God. He was, He is, and He will be.

3 … that God does not have a body. Physical concepts do not apply to Him. There is nothing that resembles Him at all.

4 … that God is first and last.

5 … that it is only proper to pray to God. One may not pray to anyone or anything else.

6 … that all the words of the prophets are true.

7 … that the prophecy of Moses is absolutely true.

8 … that the entire Torah that we now have is that which was given to Moses.

9 … that this Torah will not be changed, and that there will never be another given by God.

10 … that God knows all of man's deeds and thoughts.

11 … that God rewards those who keep His commandments, and punishes those who transgress Him.

12 … in the coming of the Messiah.

13 … that the dead will be brought back to life when God wills it to happen.

The *Jewish* way of life is

"The world stands on three things: *Torah*, worshipping God, and ACTS of kindness."
(Rabbi Shimon the Righteous, c. 300 BCE)
These ideals are the *basis* of Judaism.

The FIRST Hebrew

Judaism is one of the oldest recorded religions, existing for around 4,000 years – according to tradition, ever since God told Abraham to leave his family to become the father of a great nation. Abraham was born at a time when people worshipped idols (figures of gods made of stone or wood).

At the age of 70, Abraham made a covenant (agreement) with God, becoming the first Hebrew. Seven generations later God gave the Torah to the Jews, via the prophet Moses.

"What is hateful to *you*, do not do to Torah; the rest is commentary; go and

about?

The Star of David is called a *Magen David* (Shield of David) in Hebrew. It is said to be based on the shield used by biblical leader King David.

about *serving* GOD.

The *Torah*

The Torah (first five books of the bible) is the main Jewish scripture. It relates history from creation to the death of Moses, and describes how God wants Jews to live. The Torah is the first of three parts that make up the *Tanakh* (Hebrew Bible). The others are *Neviim* ("prophets"), and *Ketuvim* ("writings").

A religion of *ACTION*

By accepting the Torah just over 3,000 years ago, Jews agreed to follow God's commandments. There are 613 of these laws: 248 are positive ("do's") and 365 are negatives ("do not's"). They include the Ten Commandments and cover everything from how to keep the Sabbath (day of rest) to what to eat. Following the commandments brings a Jew closer to God's will.

לא תרצח   אנכי ה׳
לא תנאף   לא יהיה
לא תגנב   לא תשא
לא תענה   זכור את
לא תחמד   כבד את

The *World to Come*

Jews believe people each have a soul given to them by God. After death, the soul lives on in the World to Come (*Olam ha-Ba*). No one knows what it is truly like, but it is where the righteous are rewarded and sins are punished.

The MESSIAH

Jews also believe in the future arrival of a messiah – a leader descended from King David who will reign in an era of peace. Some think there will be a messianic *age* rather than a person. Either way, the dead will be resurrected and everyone will live in spiritual bliss.

your *neighbour*: that is the WHOLE ... LEARN it." Rabbi Hillel (1st century BCE)

DIFFERENT OPINIONS

CULTURAL differences

The Biblical Jewish homeland is Israel, although today there are more Jews living in the rest of the world. A series of exiles, starting in the 8th century BCE, saw them spread toward Europe, where two cultures evolved: Sephardi Jews of Spain and North Africa, and Ashkenazi Jews of eastern Europe. Most differences are to do with customs such as food and clothing.

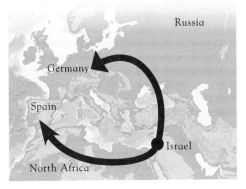

Russia

Germany

Spain

Israel

North Africa

Orthodox and Reform

Ashkenazi Jewry is split into groups, which each keep more or fewer of the commandments. It started with the Reform movement in Germany in the late 1700s. They rejected or adapted many practices so that less-observant Jews wouldn't totally abandon the religion.

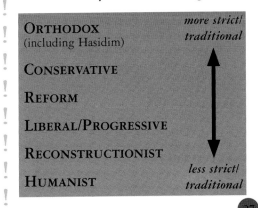

ORTHODOX (including Hasidim)	*more strict/ traditional* ↑
CONSERVATIVE	
REFORM	
LIBERAL/PROGRESSIVE	
RECONSTRUCTIONIST	
HUMANIST	*less strict/ traditional* ↓

What is CHRISTIANITY

THE *START* OF CHRISTIANITY

Christianity developed slowly from Judaism. It started around 2,000 years ago as a band of 12 disciples who followed the teachings of Jesus, but also kept Jewish practices and scriptures too. Christianity only became a separate faith when it was rejected by Jewish leaders.

The Nicene Creed

In 325 CE, the first Ecumenical council (council of bishops) set out a statement of Christian belief, which became known as the Nicene Creed. It has three parts, which profess belief first in the Father, then the Son, and then the Holy Spirit. The Nicene Creed starts:

WE BELIEVE in one God, the Father, the Almighty, maker of heaven and earth, of all that is, seen and unseen.

We believe in one Lord, Jesus Christ, the only Son of God, eternally begotten of the Father, God from God...

HEAVEN: an *eternal life* with God

Christians believe that people who turn away from sin and accept Jesus Christ will, after death, spend eternity in heaven – a place or state where God is present and there is no sin or suffering. However, all humans are naturally sinful; no one is sinless. But, through His grace (love and mercy), God forgives and grants freedom from sin to those who seek it.

Christians believe that through accepting *Jesus*

Jesus explained that the way to reach God is to have *faith* in him, and **follow** his teachings and examples – especially to *love God* with all your heart, and to *love your neighbour* as yourself.

(There are other teachings too – for example, Christians observe the Ten Commandments set out in the Old Testament of the Bible.)

The Holy *Trinity*

Christianity shares a core belief with Judaism: that there is one God. However, Christians have a unique view of God, which is that He is made up of three distinct parts.

The Holy Trinity is the Creator, Redeemer, and Guide – otherwise known as the Father, Son, and Holy Spirit.

They are not three separate gods, but together form the one God.

According to legend, Saint Patrick (373–465 CE) used a shamrock to teach how one thing can have three parts.

"Jesus said, 'I am the WAY and the to the Father *except through me.'"*

about?

The crucifix is the recognized symbol of Christianity. It represents the sacrifice Jesus made through dying on the cross to show that people can overcome sin.

SALVATION comes *Christ* as SAVIOUR.

What is *salvation*?

For Christians, salvation is returning to God. Christians believe that God created everything perfectly, but people became separated from God because of their wrongdoing. However, the Bible says that God would send a messiah to save people from their sins and bring them close to God again.

The *Fall* of humankind

The Bible teaches that Adam and Eve (the first people) committed the first sin: disobeying God by eating the forbidden fruit in the Garden of Eden. This caused the end of perfection and the Fall from grace.

And the MESSIAH is...

Christians believe the messiah is Jesus Christ. He is known as God the Son, born on Earth to the Virgin Mary. Jesus taught how to live a Christian life: love God and one another; seek God's will; and ask for forgiveness of sins.

Jesus died *for humanity*

God sacrificed His own son in order to save humanity. There are three key events surrounding the death of Jesus:

1. CRUCIFIXION
Completely innocent, Jesus was sentenced to death on a cross.

2. RESURRECTION
Three days later, Jesus appeared to some of his followers, instructing them to tell others what had happened and relate his teachings. The Resurrection shows that death and sin can be overcome.

3. ASCENSION
Forty days later, Jesus rose into heaven to be with God the Father. Christians believe that Jesus will return again at a final day of judgement to complete God's plan.

Jesus is the bridge between people and God.

PEOPLE

GOD

TRUTH and the LIFE. No one comes

New Testament book of John 14:6

CHRISTIANITY *TODAY*

More than two billion Christians belong to thousands of different denominations, which offer different styles of worship. They are usually grouped into three main categories, which have different sources of authority. Many "Protestant" churches are actually independent.

ROMAN CATHOLICISM

Officially founded in Rome in 1054
Led by the Pope, who, alongside other bishops, has authority to issue rules. Catholics believe that priests are intermediaries between people and God.

EASTERN ORTHODOX

Officially founded in Constantinople in 1054
Their focus is more on worship and humankind's good nature than on strict teachings and the nature of sin. They believe that the Holy Spirit comes from the Father only, not the Son as well.

PROTESTANT

Founded in Europe in 1500s
These churches reject the authority of the Pope, taking it from the Bible alone. The first Protestant Churches were Lutheran, Reformed and Presbyterian, and Anglican/Episcopalian. Others include Baptist, Methodist, Pentecostal, Brethren, and African Christianity.

Martin Luther

What is ISLAM

THE *FIVE PILLARS* OF ISLAM

Islam is a way of life. **The Five Pillars of Islam** are the basic requirements of Muslim life.

1 Declaring faith – *Shahada* Stating with proper intent that "There is no god but Allah" and "Muhammad is the messenger of God".

2 Prayer – *Salat*
Adult Muslims should pray five times a day: dawn, midday, late afternoon, sunset, and nightfall. The prayers are said in Arabic and include verses from the Qur'an.

3 Almsgiving – *Zakat*
Supporting the community is important, which means giving a percentage of income to charity. Additional personal contributions may also be made.

4 Fasting – *Sawm*
Ramadan is the holy month, and during daylight hours, practising Muslims who are well enough must fast (avoid eating or drinking).

5 Pilgrimage – *Hajj*
All Muslims who are physically and financially able to do so must go on a pilgrimage to Mecca in Saudi Arabia at least once in their life.

In the **Qur'an** (holy scriptures), Muslims are instructed to believe:
- there is one **God**
- He revealed **His book** – the Qur'an – to the prophet *Muhammad*
- there is a **final day of judgement**

Muhammad and the revelation
Muhammad was born in Mecca, Saudi Arabia, in c.570 CE.

In 610 CE the angel Gabriel first appeared to Muhammad and started to reveal the Qur'an – the word of God.
At that time, most people had lots of gods and idols, and felt angry to be told there was only one God. Muhammad's life was threatened, so he fled to Yathrib (later called Medina) in 622 CE. (This event, called the *Hijra*, marks the start of the Islamic calendar.) After 23 years, the Qur'an was complete.

This 16th-century painting shows Muhammad praying at the *Ka'ba*. Built in Mecca, it is Islam's holiest site.

about?

A legend reports that the founder of the Turkish Ottoman Empire (1299–1453) saw a crescent moon stretched over the whole Earth in a dream. Seeing this as a good omen, he adopted it as his Islamic empire's symbol.

to *submit* to GOD'S will, Muhammad in the *Qur'an*.

One *true* God

The message of Islam continues from the teaching of **Judaism** and **Christianity**: that there is one God (but there is no Trinity, as on page 28). The Qur'an emphasizes that "**there is no God but He**" – meaning that nothing else is like Him; He always existed, and will always exist.

The Arabic word for God is *Allah*.

Prophets of God

Muslims believe that Muhammad is the last of a line of respected prophets, which include:

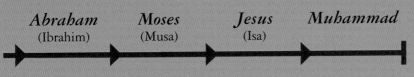

Abraham (Ibrahim)	*Moses* (Musa)	*Jesus* (Isa)	*Muhammad*

Muslims accept the teachings of all of God's messengers, but see the Qur'an as **God's final truth**.

Divine judgement

Muslims believe that God controls a person's birth, time of death, and their path through life. However, people can choose to do good things or bad things. When they die, their soul returns to God. On the **Last Day**, the end of the world, God will bring all living things to life for their final reward or punishment. Those who lived a worthy life will go to *Jannah* – "the garden of eternity". Others will be condemned to *Jahannam* (hell).

People on Earth can't really know what the afterlife is like.

DIFFERENT OPINIONS

Islam split into two different branches after the death of 'Ali, the fourth caliph (spiritual and political leader), in 661 CE.

Sunni

Around 85% of Muslims today are Sunni. After Muhammad's death, they accepted the authority of an elected caliph. There are four different Sunni schools of thought, which agree on the fundamentals of Islam, but disagree on details. Each school accepts that the others are valid, and Sunnis may choose whichever they agree with.

Shia

About 15% of Muslims are Shia. They believe that only God can choose the leader of Islam, just as only He chose Muhammad as messenger. They accepted the authority of 'Ali as divinely chosen, and called him Imam (leader) – rejecting the leadership of the three caliphs who came before him. Shias accept 'Ali's descendents as the true imams today.

Sufism

Sufis aim for a close, spiritual connection with God during their lifetime, not just in paradise. The purpose of life is to journey towards God, gaining closeness through purity. Sufism is not a separate branch of Islam, but an extra layer that may be added by any Muslim.

What is HINDUISM

FREEDOM THROUGH YOGA

Yoga comes from a Sanskrit word meaning "union". There are four main ways or paths to achieve the ultimate union (becoming one with Brahman). A Hindu may practise any, some, or all of these ways during their lifetime.

Jnana-yoga
The gaining of spiritual knowledge: learning about the relationship between the *atman* (a person's soul) and Brahman.

Dhyana- or Raja-yoga
Meditation: concentration on the real self within you so you can work towards becoming one with Brahman.

Bhakti-yoga
The worshipping of one or more of the Hindu gods, who are all in some way part of Brahman.

Karma-yoga
Knowing your duties in life and doing them correctly.

The AIM of the *Hindu* the cycle of life

HINDUISM is a collection of different traditions from the Indian subcontinent. There is no core set of *beliefs* and *practices*, but most Hindus believe in the existence of a **Supreme Power** (*Brahman*), in the **Veda** scriptures, and in the *dharma* way of life.

ONE GOD, MANY GODS
Many Hindus believe in **Brahman**. It is the power or energy that supports everything and is outside of time. Aspects of its *divine nature* are represented in other Hindu gods, who manage different parts of the *Universe* and show people the way to live.

The *Trimurti*
Some Hindus believe that the three gods of the Trimurti collectively sum up the essence of Brahman and the repetitive cycle of life. They are Brahma (the Creator), Vishnu (the Preserver), and Shiva (the Destroyer). There are many, many more Hindu gods, some of whom are the wives and children of the Trimurti. Hindus regularly pray to their personal gods and goddesses.

BRAHMA   VISHNU   SHIVA

SARASWATHI (wife of Bahma)   LAKSHMI (wife of Vishnu)   PARVATI (wife of Shiva)   GANESH (son of Shiva and Parvati)

Many Hindus call their belief system *sanatana*

about?

way of life is to escape and find *moksha*.

The *cycle* of LIFE

EVERYONE IS SUPREME

Hindus believe that there is at least part of *Brahman* in everyone. This is called the **atman**. It is distinct from the physical body and is present in every created thing, including animals and plants. (This is why all living things are treated with respect and there is a strong Hindu tradition of non-violence.) The *atman* is eternal and lives forever in a cycle of birth, death, and rebirth, called *samsara* (reincarnation).

TURNING THE CYCLE OF LIFE

Each lifetime is different from the last, depending on the *karma* of your previous life. **Karma** is a person's pursuit of good acts, spiritual knowledge, and devotion. So how people act in one life determines how their life will be when they are reborn. Hindus try to carry out good actions in one life to enable them to proceed to a better life next time round. If people choose the wrong way to live, they have to accept the consequences!

BREAKING *free*...

A person's ultimate aim is to achieve **Moksha**, which is freedom from the cycle of death and rebirth. Once they have reached the point when they realize the eternal truth, that nothing but Brahman exists, their soul unites with Brahman and lives in lasting peace and happiness.

dharma, which means "**eternal law**".

A *SPIRITUAL* JOURNEY

There are four traditional stages of life (called *ashrama*) for a Hindu, and four goals (*purusharthas*) to follow along the way. Many Hindus today see these stages and goals as ideals rather than as something to adhere to strictly.

1 Brahmacarya
The student stage. Aged five, a child goes to live with a guru to study scriptures, meditate, and learn self-discipline. The first goal starts now and remains central throughout life: following the moral code, or *dharma*.

2 Grihastha
The householder stage, when a man should marry and start a family. Stages 2 and 3 have two additional goals: the pursuit of success and wealth, and of love and pleasure.

3 Vanaprastha
The retirement stage. Sons take over the household so the father is free to focus on his death and rebirth. This may involve more active worship of the gods, or a withdrawal from life.

4 Sannyasa
Life and all it entails is given up in order to search for the fourth goal: *moksha* (freedom from reincarnation and unity with Brahman).

What is BUDDHISM

THE *BUDDHIST* WAY OF LIFE

The *Five* Precepts

After accepting the Three Jewels, Buddhists undertake to follow the Five Precepts as taught by the Buddha.

1. Do not kill
2. Do not steal
3. Do not indulge in sexual misconduct
4. Do not make false speech
5. Do not take intoxicants

The *Noble Eightfold Path*

This spiritual path enables Buddhists to develop wisdom and reach *nirvana*.

Right view (*samma ditthi*) – seeing the world clearly by understanding the Four Noble Truths.

Right thought (*samma sankappa*) – being compassionate and not causing harm or upset to others.

Right speech (*samma vaca*) – being truthful, not gossiping or saying anything that is harmful or boastful.

Right action (*samma kammanta*) – living a moral life and having respect for all living creatures.

Right livelihood (*samma ajiva*) – choosing an ethical job.

Right effort (*samma vayama*) – making a conscious effort to leave behind negative emotions, actions, and states of being.

Right mindfulness (*samma sati*) – thinking clearly and being fully aware of thoughts, usually through meditation.

Right concentration (*samma samadhi*) – focussing on becoming detached from the material world in order to focus on the inward path to enlightenment.

The **basis** of Buddhist life is *accepting DHARMA* (the Buddha's teachings), and

THE BUDDHA

Buddhism is based on the teachings of *Siddhartha Gautama*. Troubled by the poverty and suffering he saw, he gave up all worldly goods (even food) and *meditated* on the problem. His mind was awoken to the truths of the Universe, and he became the Buddha – a title that means "*the Enlightened One*".

> I lived in northern India 2,500 years ago.

THE FOUR NOBLE TRUTHS

After finding enlightenment, the Buddha preached the truths he had discovered. These became known as the Four Noble Truths.

1. *Dukkha* – All life involves suffering, stress, and ageing. All life ends in death.

2. *Samudaya* – Suffering is caused by negative thoughts, by craving things, and by people trying to control the world around them.

3. *Nirodha* – Suffering has an end. This is called *nirvana*.

4. *Magga* – *Nirvana* can be reached by following the Noble Eightfold Path.

enlightenment.

Buddhism differs to other religions in that

about?

The *Dharmachakra* (wheel of life) symbolizes the circle of life, death, and rebirth. Its eight spokes represent the Noble Eightfold Path.

the *Three Jewels*: the BUDDHA, SANGHA (Buddhist community).

THE CIRCLE OF LIFE
Reincarnation and *karma*

Buddhists believe that each time they die, they are reborn in another life. How they are reborn depends on how they have behaved in their past lives. This is controlled by a life force called *karma*. If they have lived good lives, their *karma* will be good and they will be reborn to an easier life – one where there is less suffering. But if they have expressed negative thoughts and actions, they will be reborn to a harder life.

A Buddhist escapes the circle of life of life through

Nirvana

The goal of the Buddhist path is to break free from the cycle of rebirth. Suffering happens when people don't accept that everything, including themselves, is impermanent. *Nirvana* is the real understanding and experience that everything is impermanent. This state of blissful enlightenment brings about an end to suffering, struggling, and worldly desires, and marks the end of the cycle of life, death, and rebirth.

THE *SANGHA*

The Buddha created a *community* of monks and nuns who rely on charity from the rest of the people. By giving up worldly things, their way of life demonstrates to others that everyone must undergo a *transformation* to find **enlightenment**.

there is no **BELIEF** in a higher power (ie God).

DIFFERENT OPINIONS

There are two main branches of Buddhism: Theravada is a monastic tradition, and Mahayana is more a vision of what Buddhism is really about. Both have many schools and traditions across different countries.

Theravada Buddhism

Theravada means the "doctrine of the elders" and is thought to be the oldest branch of Buddhism. Theravadans accept that there have been other Buddhas, but they revere Siddhartha Gautama as the supreme Buddha because he reached nirvana without guidance from others. Theravada Buddhists believe that enlightenment can only be achieved through their own efforts, and not through their belief in the Buddha alone.

Mahayana Buddhism

Most Mahayana Buddhists suggest that the ultimate goal is not simply to reach nirvana, but also to help others to do so. Mahayana Buddhism is split into two main groups: Tibetan Buddhism and East Asian Mahayana (which is further divided into Pure Land Buddhism and Zen Buddhism).

Buddhism in the world

Buddhism is popular across the world today in a "westernized" form. In Asia, Buddhism focusses less on the individual and more on community.

What is SIKHISM

SIKH BELIEFS

The *Mool Mantar*

The *Mool Mantar* mantra (prayer) describes the nature of God and forms the basis of Sikh belief. It is recited every morning on waking, so a Sikh starts his or her day having God in mind.

There is only ONE GOD;
Truth is His Name;
He is the Creator;
He is without fear;
He is without hate;
He is timeless, without form;
He is beyond birth and death,
The ENLIGHTENED one;
He can be known by The Guru's Grace.

Virtues and vices

In order to reach liberation (*mukti*) and achieve union with God, people must try to follow the **five virtues** and remove the **five human vices,** which make them self-centred and build a barrier between them and God.

Increase virtue:	*Reduce vice:*
TRUTH	LUST
COMPASSION	ANGER
CONTENTMENT	GREED
HUMILITY	ATTACHMENT TO WORLDLY THINGS
LOVE OF GOD	
	PRIDE (EGO)

LIBERATION in this life

It is possible to achieve union with God in this life, although few people achieve it. This is called *Jeevan Mukt.*

A Sikh has THREE duties at all times; earn an *honest*

THE *START* OF SIKHISM

Guru Nanak was born in 1469 in India. A Hindu poet and philosopher, he founded Sikhism after years of studying Hinduism and Islam and debating with holy men. His teachings centred on the importance of living a God-centred life and a person's inner soul, rather than focusing on rituals and external signs of faith, such as penance.

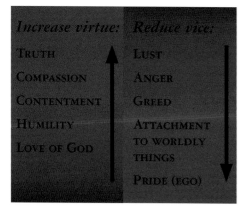

Guru Nanak
1469–1539

The Ten Gurus

Sikhism is sometimes called *Gurmat* ("the Guru's doctrine") because the teachings of the Gurus show the right way to live. God is seen as the original Guru, and He chose the first Guru, Nanak. There were nine more Gurus, each one chosen by the one before for their spiritual insight and moral perfection. The Tenth Guru, Gobind Singh, stated that he would be the last human Guru: after he died in 1708, the eleventh Guru would be the holy book *Granth Sahib,* which remains the Sikh authority today.

Guru Angad

Guru Amar Das

Guru Ram Das

Guru Arjan

Guru Hargobind

The word SIKH comes from the **Sanskrit** word

The Khanda contains three symbols:
khanda (double-edged sword) = morality, justice, and God's power over all;
chakra (the circle) = one never-ending God;
kirpan (two curved swords) = balance of spiritual and political power.

about?

in life: *have God in mind living*; and give to *charity*.

The ONE God

Sikhs believe in one God, without form or gender. He is *sargun* (everywhere and in everything) and *nirgun* (above and beyond creation). God created the world and people and is in everyone's soul, therefore all have direct access to God and everyone is equal before him.

The *Ik Onkar* symbol means "one God".

The *inner self*

Sikhism stresses the importance of a person's inner religious self and good actions over rituals. In order to live a good life, a person must keep God in their heart and mind at all times. They should live as part of a community, living honestly and working hard, treating everyone equally, helping those less fortunate than themselves, and serving others.

Liberation...

The aim of a Sikh is for their soul to eventually become one with God. To do this they must focus away from themselves and focus on God and living a God-centred life. This freeing of the soul from the body at death is called *mukti* (liberation).

... Or reincarnation

A person who is self-centred during life will suffer in heavens and hells after death, before being reincarnated as another species. Their soul will be reborn again and again until it is in human form, when it will have another chance to achieve *mukti*.

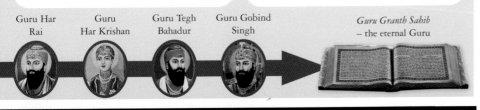

Guru Har Rai   Guru Har Krishan   Guru Tegh Bahadur   Guru Gobind Singh   *Guru Granth Sahib* – the eternal Guru

shishya, which means "disciple" or "one who learns".

SIKH LIFE

COMMUNITY living

Being a Sikh means using everyday actions as a way of reaching God. Religious rituals are meaningless unless you live a good life and care for other people. Sikh life revolves around the community – belonging to the *Khalsa*; caring for the poor or sick; providing community meals (called *langar*); and performing chores at a *Gurdwara* (house of worship). By serving others, a Sikh can get rid of the ego that blocks them from getting close to God. It is also a reminder that everyone is equal, and everyone has God within them.

The *Khalsa*

In 1699 Guru Gobind Singh created the idea of a community of Sikhs called the *Khalsa Panth*, the "soldier saints". All who chose to join the *Khalsa Panth* and dedicate their lives to Sikhism were required to wear five physical symbols, the five Ks, to show their membership (see page 62). The *Khalsa* today is made up of initiated Sikhs. Not all Sikhs have to belong to it, but they still may wear some of the five K's to show their Sikh identity.

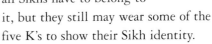

Native religions

Native (or more accurately, indigenous) people include not only African, Aboriginal, South American, Inuit, and Native American, but also Norse shamans and the Foe of Papua New Guinea. They tend to have an *instinctive*, underlying spirituality that is part of their *everyday life*.

Here are some examples of native religious groups:

AFRICAN TRIBES

African tribes generally have a family-based and practical spirituality, so they carry out rituals and ceremonies to make their community healthy and prosperous. They don't have formal guidelines, and their practices often adapt to outside influences.

Rituals

There are rituals (which may involve animal sacrifice, music, and dancing) to celebrate new year and harvest, as well as birth, marriage and death. Coming of age and initiation rites might include body marking or scarring, and carrying out particular tasks such as hunting. Another important focus of tribal ritual is to gain the cooperation and favour of ancestors and other spirits, and to create harmony with them.

Explaining life

Masks often represent ancestral spirits.

Traditional stories explain misfortune and illness. Many refer to a time before living memory, when people and gods lived in harmony until people messed up – maybe by quarrelling – and were punished. Mostly, death is seen as the gateway to an afterlife as an ancestor. The quality of this afterlife depends on how, and how much, each person is remembered by the living.

The Ashanti people of Ghana have a clear concept of **reincarnation**. They believe people come back time and time again until they finish what they were meant to do on Earth, then they move on to enter the world of the ancestors.

THE FROZEN NORTH

The tribes of the Arctic (such as the Inuit in Canada, and the Chukchi and Nenets in Siberia) share many things – bitter cold and near starvation, as well as religious beliefs.

Arctic Circle

KEY teachings

Based on the theory that all creatures, not just people, have souls, Arctic tribes follow an elaborate system of ritual to ensure that animals are available to hunters. For each species of land animal, there is a Master or Keeper, and an underwater goddess controls fish and sea mammals. According to how closely the tribe follows their rituals, these spirits release or withhold the animals in their charge.

Guides for the spirit

Shaman mask

Arctic tribes often have spiritual leaders called shamans. They communicate between the human and the spirit worlds, interpreting the causes of any disease or lack of success in hunting, and suggesting an appropriate way to make things right. To do this, shamans often use chanting and drums to enter into the trance state that gives access to their special knowledge and power.

The Inuit believe in **eternal life**, but it takes more than a year to pass from this life into the afterlife. To make this journey, the soul crawls under an enormous animal-skin carpet.

They don't consider this spirituality to be a "religion" in the way some cultures do, but many have beliefs and practices in common:

Respect. Honouring significant figures, spirits, or objects brings comfort. Those honoured include gods, ancestors (who are physically dead but still powerful), elders, priests, and other living people. Animals, plants, clouds, and sacred sites are also respected.

Rituals to honour significant figures. The theory is that when these figures are happy, people's lives will be better. Often, rituals are conducted by a respected elder such as a shaman (part priest, part magician, part doctor) who is believed to have special powers.

Giving. The exchanging of gifts with each other is a meaningful part of life, and the offering of gifts to significant beings or objects is an important sign of love and respect.

NATIVE AMERICANS

Native American tribes are all different, but they all believe that everything in life is part of one whole, which they see as a big circle – at its centre, life is created by One Great Spirit. Being part of a whole in this way affects the way people understand the world – light and dark, hot and cold, etc are not seen as opposites, but as balances to each other. All relationships – with people and with nature – are about give and take.

On the north Pacific coast, where trees grow tall and strong, indigenous tribes carve tall **totem poles** from them. These use animal or human figures to record tribal legends, clan relationships, or important events.

All about NATURE

Historically, tribes lived with nature, and their beliefs involved related spirits – of rain, Sun, etc. The complexity of each system varied with the tribe's way of life. The Iroquois, for example, lived in the fertile northeast woods where food was easy to find, so they had the time to develop sophisticated ideas about the One Great Spirit, lots of lesser spirits, and an Evil Spirit. The Iroquois believe that people have an eternal soul.

Struggling to *survive*

The Apaches in the barren southwest are much more concerned with survival. They have few resources for ritual – no marriage ceremony was developed, and there is no formal belief in an afterlife. Individuals establish their own relationships with nature and the supernatural.

It's hard to find food in Arizona's dry landscape.

ABORIGINES

During the 19th century, Christian missionaries travelled widely throughout Australia, and their religion came to be accepted by many Aborigines. Today, although original beliefs and practices are still alive, more than two-thirds of Australian Aborigines are Christians.

Traditional Aboriginal thinking is centred on the belief that all creation took place in another order of time that is separate from our ideas of past and present. This is known as Dreamtime – a term that is sometimes translated as "everywhen". There were a number of gods, most of which were represented by something real – an animal, a plant, or even a rock. All these spirits, sometimes called Ancestral Beings, had their own creation story. They all made their own contribution to the world, including guidelines for people to follow.

Native American totem pole

EAST ASIAN *religions*

CONFUCIANISM

After Confucius died, his ideas and writings were so revered in China that they become a religion. In the 1st century BCE, this became the state religion, and it held its place until the 20th century. Confucianism is still followed by millions in Asia.

Confucius, 552–479 BCE

Main teachings

Based on principles of harmony, tolerance, and excellence, Confucianism offers guidelines for creating successful people, families, and societies. Confucius wanted people to love and respect others (especially elders and superiors), to do good, and to honour tradition. He recommended two ways of achieving these things – the principles of *ren* (humane behaviour) and *Li* (manners, ceremony, and ritual).

TAOISM

Taoism is based on the writings of two philosophers, Laozi and Zhuangzi, who taught that Tao ("the Way") is the principle controlling the Universe. It became a religion in the 2nd century BCE, and later absorbed other sects and practices.

Taoist leaders

The key teachings

Taoism is an inward-looking faith, but it also focuses on ritual worship and divination. Like Confucianism, it's concerned with yin and yang, and stresses the importance of harmony with the Universe, and consideration for others. Taoists believe its practices not only enhance life, but also help people reach Heaven, where they become immortals.

SHINTO

In China and Japan, there are *many different* gods and spirits, and lots of different traditions mixed together. The best-known belief systems are *Confucianism* and *Taoism*, which originated in China, and *Shinto*, from Japan. **Buddhism** (see page 34) is also important in east Asia.

What about GOD?

Confucianism doesn't have a single God-like figure – it suggests the existence of an ultimate, unknowable force called *Taiji*, which controls the universe and the human spirit. But there are lots of lesser gods, spirits, and ancestors who live in Heaven. These are worshipped by the people, who turn to them with requests – for fruitful harvests, for example, or recovery from illness.

YIN/YANG

Many Asian faiths teach the principle of yin (dark, moist, soft, cold, feminine) and yang (light, dry, hard, warm, masculine). Everything has yin and yang qualities in different proportions, and the ultimate goal is to achieve harmony by keeping them in balance.

CHINESE POPULAR RELIGION

This blend of Confucianism, Taoism, and Buddhism is practised by the Chinese around the world. It stresses community festivals, the worship of immortals, and rituals like temple offerings and incense burning.

T'ai chi

Taoism helps people understand the energy or life-force (*chi* or *qi*) that flows through channels in the body and connects all living things. The graceful movements of t'ai-chi are not just for exercise, but also to help the *chi* flow freely. When this happens, all inner strength and energy are brought together and released.

Shinto practices

People visit shrines or holidays or to make a wish. The focus of Shinto is ritual rather than prayer, so believers wash before entering the shrine to make sure they are pure. Many ancient Shinto practices are preserved in Buddhist temples.

Shinto teachings

Like Shinto itself means "way of the kami", the spirits of Shinto. Shinto encourages people to live in harmony with the world and be happy and positive. Part of this is to help humans achieve this goal, humans live a kind of worship called *the kami*.

MIX and *match*

Shinto naturally combines with other faiths. Part of Japan, Buddhism, and other faiths. This is a good example of how different religions work together. The Japanese combine Shinto, Buddhism, and folk traditions in every part of life. When they're born, babies are blessed at a Shinto shrine and placed under the *kami's* protection; at death, the subject to Buddhist rites. So most Japanese are "born Shinto and die Buddhist".

Sumo wrestling

Sumo, whose origins are linked to Shinto, dates back many centuries. Early matches took place at Shinto shrines to please the *kami*, and they were sponsored by the court to ensure good harvests.

NEW RELIGIOUS

INTRODUCING SOME NRMs

Bahai
Founded in: Tehran, Iran, 1863
Founder: Mirza Husayn-Ali Nuri, the Baha'u'llah
Number of followers: 5–7 million

Cao Dai
Founded in: Vietnam, 1926
Founder: Ngu Van Chieu
Number of followers: 8 million

Church of Christ, Scientist (Christian Science)
Founded in: Massachusetts, USA, 1879
Founder: Mary Baker Eddy
Number of followers: 400,000

Church of Jesus Christ of Latter-day Saints (Mormons)
Founded in: New York, USA, 1830
Founder: Joseph Smith Jr
Number of followers: 12–13 million

Falun Gong
Founded in: China, 1992
Founder: Li Hongzhi
Number of followers: 10 million

Family Federation for World Peace and Unification (Moonies)
Founded in: South Korea, 1954
Founder: Sun Myung Moon
Number of followers: 250,000–1 million

Religions are often thought of as being part of a family's *tradition* or *culture* for **many generations**. However, there are hundreds of new religious movements that have sprung up in the last 180 years all over the world.

New **religion**, new **ideas**

Many NRMs are based in established world religions; however, some are entirely original. Scientology was started by L. Ron Hubbard, who believed that each person has an immortal spirit (called the thetan) with unlimited capabilities. However, the thetan is harmed by experiences in life (called engrams) and it must be cleansed through spiritual counselling (called auditing) to reach salvation.

L. Ron Hubbard's books, lectures, and films form the scriptures of Scientology.

FOLLOWING IN THE *FOOTSTEPS*

Many NRMs are derived from an existing world religion, although some

Holding to *Hinduism*
ISKCON (also known as Hare Krishna) is derived from Hinduism but worships Krishna as the main god having Supreme Power. Like many other Hindus, they believe in reincarnation, and their main scriptures are the *Vedas*. However, the ISKCON way of life focuses on *bhakti* (service to Krishna), especially through chanting and *bhakti-yoga*.

Statue of A.C. Bhaktivedanta Swami Prabhupada.

Coming from *Christianity*
Jehovah's Witnesses, the Church of Jesus Christ of Latter-day Saints (Mormons), and Christian Science are just some of many Christian-based NRMs. However, they are not always accepted as "official" Christian denominations because their teachings are too different from mainstream Christianity – for example, they all reject the idea of the Trinity.

Brigham Young, an early Mormon leader.

MOVEMENTS (NRMS)

WHY START A RELIGION?

Like the established world religions, many **NRMs** (but not all) are founded by people who believe they have received a *revelation* from God that replaces or fulfils an earlier one. (At least, most *prophets* get their revelation from God; the **Buddha**, for example, came to his own enlightenment through meditation.)

Spreading the *WORD*

"Health is not a condition of matter, but of Mind."

Mary Baker Eddy started **The Church of Christ (Scientist)** after being cured of a serious injury without medical help. While reading a biblical story of Jesus healing, she realized that healing came through spiritual means. Suddenly she was cured, and went on to teach that physical and spiritual health came from knowing God.

have evolved very different ideas. Here are just a few examples.

It started with *Islam*

Siyyid 'Ali-Muhammad, who paved the way for the Bahai faith, was brought up a Muslim. He received a revelation that Islam was not the final will of God, but that His message would continue through another prophet to come in the future. The prophet he foretold of was Baha'u'llah, founder of the Bahai faith.

Bahai Shrine of The Bab in Haifa, Israel.

Based in *Buddhism*

Soka Gakkai International (SGI) is based on the teachings of Nichiren, a 13th-century Japanese Buddhist monk. He taught that all people possess the Buddha nature and so can learn positive lessons from any situation to live a happy, fulfilled life. SGI says that when one person makes an inner change, it affects the whole world in a positive way.

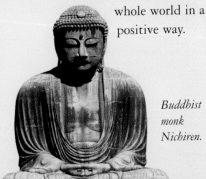

Buddhist monk Nichiren.

International Society for Krishna Consciousness (ISKCON)

Founded in: New York, USA, 1966
Founder: Bhaktivedanta Swami Prabhupada
Number of followers: 250,000–1 million

Jehovah's Witnesses

Founded in: Pittsburgh, USA, 1879
Founder: Charles Taze Russell
Number of followers: 6.5 million

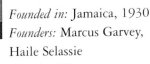

Rastafarianism

Founded in: Jamaica, 1930
Founders: Marcus Garvey, Haile Selassie
Number of followers: 1 million

Scientology

Founded in: California, USA, 1954
Founder: L. Ron Hubbard
Number of followers: 70,000–millions

Soka Gakkai International (SGI)

Founded in: Japan, 1930
Founder: Tsunesaburo Makiguchi
Number of followers: 12 million

Cults

NRMs used to be called cults, but today the word cult has a negative meaning, suggesting a threat to "normal life" perhaps by brainwashing its followers or cutting them off from their family. Most NRMs are not like this. However, cults do exist in the form of "doomsday" religious groups (those that believe ending life will bring about salvation).

MODERN

During the last half of the 20th century, especially in the wealthy West, more and more people turned away from *traditional* religion. Yet many people still felt the need for a **modern** spirituality in which rules and rituals are replaced by *sensitivity* to natural *energies*, awareness of self and others, and the search for *peace* and well-being.

GAZING *IN*

The importance of personal development or "self" is one of the central focuses of modern spirituality. This isn't about being selfish – instead, it's about listening to your own spiritual voice in order to find enlightenment. In modern spirituality, "life" rather than "God" is sacred – life must be appreciated, and lived to its full potential.

> MIND, body, *spirit*

Meditation is often done in yoga poses.

Personal path

Freedom and independence are also central. To be true to "life", people must follow their own path, without rules that might limit their freedom and hinder self-discovery. The stresses of the world can throw lives out of balance, and spirituality is concerned with restoring the vital balance of mind, body, and spirit.

Pick and mix

Modern spirituality is "this-worldly" rather than "other worldly", and more concerned with earthly life than afterlife. This spirituality has no general teachings or practices – individuals either develop their own beliefs, adopt and adapt teachings from existing systems, or do both.

Spirituality offers an escape from the stresses of life.

Spirituality provides a middle way between traditional

Spirituality

LOOKING *EAST*

Eastern religions such as **Buddhism** and **Taoism** often inspire those in search of personal fulfillment. Also, these systems stress the importance of harmony with the Universe, an important element in modern spirituality. But Eastern practices adopted in the West are greatly changed and adapted from their original sacred teachings and doctrines – in modern spirituality, they are freed from religious meaning.

EAST

To some people, the Buddha represents serenity.

Meditation

In its many forms, meditation is a form of mental discipline designed to regulate and harmonize mind and body. The aim is usually to promote well-being and encourage calm, awareness, clear-headedness, concentration, and deep relaxation. Many types of meditation involve specific techniques, which may require repeating a word, or assuming a special position.

Yoga

The word "yoga" (meaning "to control or unite") refers to various physical and mental disciplines that originated in India. Hinduism, Jainism, and Buddhism all involve yoga-related practices. These involve a range of physical positions and many are to do with spiritual well-being.

Feng shui

This ancient Chinese discipline (the name means "wind and water") is aimed at creating harmony by the careful placing of objects around us. Good feng shui is thought to capture and strengthen chi (natural energy). Followers believe it removes or deflects things that block it. By this means, harmony with nature is achieved peaceful, and resonates with Tao. Feng shui is used in planning, building, and furnishing homes and offices.

Feng shui in practice

A room with good feng shui is free of beams, columns and projecting angles that interrupt the flow of *chi*. Healthy plants symbolize nature and encourage the flow of *chi*, while wilted plants or flowers have a negative effect. Colour too is important – green is associated with tranquility, red with strength, and yellow and orange with confidence.

religion and empty non-belief.

What is ATHEISM

The word *atheism* comes from the Greek words *a* (which means "**without**") and *theos* (meaning "**god**").

ATHEISM can be interpreted in many ways. The belief at the heart of atheism is that there is *no such thing as God or gods*. In some people, this is an active denial; in others, it simply means the absence of belief in God.

The different levels of atheism:

> I believe that God or gods do not exist.

> I don't believe in God or gods, but I don't deny that He/they exist.

DENIAL ← → DISBELIEF

NON-THEISM

 Buddhism, Confucianism, and Taoism are non-theistic religions: they do not believe in a main creator God (although some Buddhists believe in lesser gods and spirits). But they are not technically atheist, because atheism doesn't really apply to Eastern religions – it is a western response to monotheism.

SOME FORMS OF ATHEISM:

Humanism

Humanists believe that the source of all truth and values is found within humans – it does not come through a revelation from God, nor is religion necessary to teach morals. Humanists say there is no afterlife: this world is all there is, so people should behave morally here and now.

Rationalism

Rationalists say that all beliefs should be tested by reason and science, and only those that are justified by rational argument and scientific evidence should be accepted. A rationalist would say that there is no evidence for God, so a person should be atheist or agnostic.

What is agnosticism?

I coined the term "agnostic" from the Greek for *not knowable*. The claims of atheism are too definite – it's just not possible to truly know if God exists or not. And as the question of God's existence is unanswerable, we shouldn't answer it.

NOT *JUST* NOT KNOWING

Agnosticism does not simply mean that a person is unsure about God. Rather, it is the belief that there is not enough information and so one should not make a decision.

Thomas Henry Huxley *1860*

about?

The "Happy Human" is the symbol of the International Humanist and Ethical Union.

I'm not religious. Does that make me an *atheist*?

Is atheism a religion?

In a word, no. But an atheist may still follow a code for life. For example, humanists abide by certain moral beliefs (usually based on the value of human life) and have rituals such as humanist weddings and funerals. There are also humanists within mainstream religions (such as Jewish Humanists) who do not accept the existence of a creator God, but still follow other aspects of the religion's culture or practices.

Religion doesn't enter some people's lives at all. They don't necessarily deny that God exists because they don't even think about God to accept or deny Him. This would make them a "weak" atheist, which also overlaps with some forms of agnosticism.

Secularism

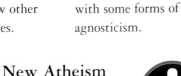

Secularists say that society should not be influenced by religion. Many feel that people can be free to practice religion in their own home (some may even do so themselves as not all secularists are atheist), but they would ban public displays such as prayers in school.

New Atheism

The New Atheism movement started in 2004, based on books by the authors Richard Dawkins, Daniel Dennett, Sam Harris, and Christopher Hitchens. They are anti-religion, saying that science and logic should be used to disprove religion.

TYPES OF AGNOSTICISM:

STRONG AGNOSTICISM – No one can ever truly know whether God or gods exist – there's just not enough evidence to know, and never will be.

WEAK AGNOSTICISM – I don't yet know whether God or gods exist, but we might find out in the future.

AGNOSTIC THEISM – I believe in God but have no proof He definitely exists. Or, I believe in God but I don't know anything about Him.

AGNOSTIC ATHEISM – I don't believe in God, but I have no proof that He definitely does not exist.

ATHEISM: A BRIEF HISTORY

Greek ORIGINS

Atheism is said to have started in ancient Greece, where it was a crime not to accept the state gods. However, strong atheism – the denial of the existence of gods – was very rare.

Modern atheists

Strong atheism comes from modern Western thinking. Sparked by the Enlightenment in the 17th century, modern atheism challenged the authority of the Church. Academics questioned the authorship and realism of stories in the Bible; and science began to replace religion as a means of providing answers.

In *1841*, philosopher **Ludwig Feuerbach** said that God did not exist, but that He was invented by people as a way of understanding life's purpose.

In *1844*, **Karl Marx** wrote that "man creates religion, religion does not create man". He called religion "opium" – meaning that it kept people suppressed.

I say **"GOD IS DEAD"**.
(What I mean is, people have killed off God by no longer believing in Him.)

Friedrich Nietzsche, *1882*

In *1859*, **Charles Darwin** published his theory of evolution. It undermined religious explanations of the creation, but he felt that a person could believe in God *and* evolution.

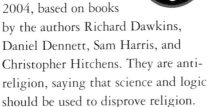

Festivals and *rituals* remind me of what – and who – is important.
I honour my god through colourful *offerings*.
Shh! I'm trying to concentrate on *praying!*

? WHY do *you*...?

As a *novice monk,* I have a lot to learn.

There's *more* to religion than **belief**.

For most people, religion is not just about what they *think*, but what they DO. It can impact upon what they wear, what they eat, what they say – in fact, **almost everything** a person does can be influenced by their religion.

But what are religious practices *actually about*? What do they **mean** to the person doing them? And *where* do they come from?

You've read the teachings. You've heard the ideas. Now see religion in action!

The GOOD BOOKS

WHAT ARE SCRIPTURES?

The holy books of a religion contain the words, thoughts, and deeds of religious leaders and teachers, or even of God Himself. Many scriptures were originally oral (spoken), but were later written down. This helps to preserve them and keep the teachings consistent, especially when religions spread across the world.

The Buddhist *Tipitaka* contains the teachings of the Buddha.

WHO ARE YOU TO TELL ME WHAT TO DO?

In most cases, scriptures are generally accepted to be inspired or revealed by God. For example, the Qur'an is the words of God revealed to Muhammad. Some people challenge whether texts are written by God (or His messengers), although it is probably not provable either way. However, believers accept the scriptures' authority, and that is what is important. Poems and commentaries also come from people who have either been divinely inspired or reached their own enlightenment, giving them the authority to teach the masses.

The Gospels of Matthew, Mark, Luke, and John in the New Testament take their authority from being accounts of the life and works of Jesus.

USING THE SCRIPTURES

People turn to the scriptures to get answers to life's big questions and also for the everyday details of life: how to behave, what to eat – and what happens if we disobey. However, it's not always easy to find the rules among the stories, and so some religions have other texts and commentaries to explain the rules in more detail.

The 36 books of Talmud record rabbis' discussions of Jewish law. It took 600 years to compile and is still studied today.

Section of law

Discussions about the section

JUDAISM
Name: Tanakh (sometimes called the Hebrew Bible)
Contents: 24 books in three sections:
Torah – the five books of Moses
Neviim – "prophets"
Ketuvim – "writings"
Language: Hebrew; some Aramaic
Date: 1313 BCE–6th century BCE

BUDDHISM
Name: Tipitaka
Contents: Three "baskets":
Vinaya Pitaka – rules for monks and nuns
Sutta Pitaka – the Buddha's main teachings
Abhidhamma Pitaka – how to use teachings
Language: Pali
Date: originally oral, first written down 3rd–1st century BCE

HINDUISM
Two types of text:
Shruti ("things heard") are the words of gods revealed to scholars and includes the *Vedas*; and
Smrti ("things remembered") written to teach laws, rituals, and mythology
Language: Sanskrit
Date: oldest *Veda* from c. 1500 BCE

A religion's beliefs, rules, and regulations come from its scriptures – texts that provide MEANING and GUIDANCE for believers. Scriptures can be of many **different** kinds: teachings, laws, stories, poetry, and history.

In the *Bhagavad Gita*, the Hindu deity Krishna (disguised as a chariot driver) instructs a reluctant warrior that it is his duty to fight, teaching that every person must fulfil their life's purpose.

THE MORAL OF THE STORY

Often scriptural teachings are presented through the retelling of historical events, showing how the religion itself developed. Some teachings are presented as stories (or parables), making them more easily understood and remembered. Sometimes believers debate whether a particular text would be best understood as an historical account or as a parable.

HOLY WORDS, HOLY BOOK

In most religions, the books (or scrolls) themselves are treated as holy objects because they contain the words of God. They would never be put on the floor or casually thrown away. Hand-written copies of the Qur'an (known as *mushaf*) are carefully copied so that none of God's words are changed. A *mushaf* may be ornately decorated using calligraphy and patterns, but not pictures of people or animals – that could be seen as idolatry, which is strictly forbidden.

KNOWLEDGE FOR ALL

Reading from the scriptures is an essential part of prayer services or other forms of worship, providing believers with lessons on how to live and reminding them Who's in charge. Reading the text aloud makes it more accessible for everyone to hear; and if the words are chanted, they are easier to remember – just like if you hear a favourite song two years after you last heard it, you will remember at least some of the words.

The Sikh *Guru Granth Sahib* is read aloud by a Granthi (a temple official), who may be a man or a woman.

A Qur'an made today reads the same as one written a thousand years ago.

ISLAM
Name: Qur'an
Contents: 114 chapters (*suras*) that are the words of Allah as revealed to Muhammad
Language: Arabic
Date: revealed 610–632 CE; originally memorized but first written down c. 650 CE

CHRISTIANITY
Name: Bible
Contents: Old Testament (a variation on the Hebrew Bible), and New Testament (27 books, including the four Gospels)
Language: Hebrew and Aramaic; Greek (translated into Latin in the 14th century)
Date: Written at different times, but completed by 95–150 CE

SIKHISM
Name: **Adi Granth** (official name); more often called **Guru Granth Sahib**
Contents: 1430 pages of hymns written by the Gurus and non-gurus
Language: Gurmukhi (a written form of Punjabi)
Date: first compiled in 1604; revised and completed c. 1700

What's the POINT of PRAYER?

THE *ELEMENTS* OF PRAYER

Prayers in every religion have elements in common: praise, request, and confession. Thanksgiving often goes with request – after all, it's only polite to say thanks when you've asked God for something!

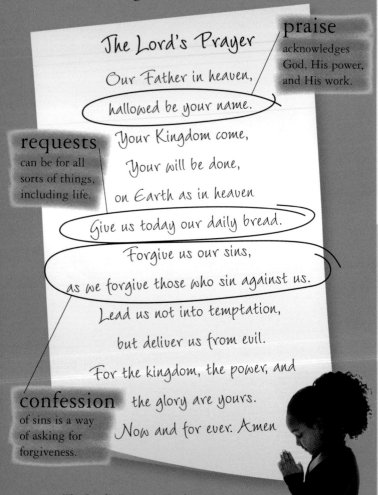

The Lord's Prayer

Our Father in heaven,

hallowed be your name.

Your Kingdom come,

Your will be done,

on Earth as in heaven

Give us today our daily bread.

Forgive us our sins,

as we forgive those who sin against us.

Lead us not into temptation,

but deliver us from evil.

For the kingdom, the power, and the glory are yours.

Now and for ever. Amen

praise
acknowledges God, His power, and His work.

requests
can be for all sorts of things, including life.

confession
of sins is a way of asking for forgiveness.

The Lord's Prayer is the key prayer in Christianity. It was taught by Jesus to his disciples, and appears twice in the New Testament.

PRAYER IS...

Ritual

Prayer is a religious action, or ritual. It was the first practice of ISLAM, as the Qur'an records the prophet Muhammad being instructed by God to pray twice a day. Muslims today are called to prayer five times a day. The rules of prayer are laid out in the *shari'a* (Islamic code of law). They include things like the wording of prayer, and how to hold your hands.

Public and private

There are three daily prayer services in JUDAISM, which are best performed with a *minyan*, or congregation of at least 10 adults (10 men in Orthodox Judaism). If people cannot find a *minyan*, they may still pray, but will have to leave out certain prayers. There are also personal, private prayers and blessings that are said during the day.

Imagine being able to *phone* God. You could make **requests**, ask Him QUESTIONS, and hear His *answers*. Unfortunately not even the best satellite communications have managed this (yet) – but for believers, there is a *hotline* to Him. This is **PRAYER**.

Devotion

Prayers called mantras are a part of HINDU devotion – a way of expressing love for God. Most Hindus worship at a home shrine, where they make offerings, light lamps and incense, and chant mantras. A mantra is as much a sound as it is a prayer: it summons the deity's attention.

A Hindu family prepares offerings at an outdoor *puja* (worship) ceremony.

Spiritual development

Simran is the active remembrance of the core SIKH belief that there is one God. *Simran* includes meditating and reciting the daily *Mool Mantar* prayer. It reminds people of all the aspects of God and acknowledges His power in the world.

Prayer in *action*

Tibetan Buddhists recite mantras to help them concentrate. Mantras are also written on flags, or on paper inside prayer wheels. When the flags flutter or the wheels turn, it's like repeating a mantra over and over.

WHO is prayer for?

Monotheistic religions believe that God is all-powerful. So why does He need our prayers? One explanation is that He doesn't *need* them, but is glad to receive them in the same way your mum or dad likes it when you say thank you. God too wants the best for His children, but sometimes they take things for granted. Prayers are a reminder of God. So you could say that prayer is not for Him, but for the believer.

More than *words*

There may be psychological benefits to prayer: it focuses your mind; it gives you "time out"; and provides comfort. Sometimes prayer can seem like a one-way phone call to God: you're doing all the talking, but you can't hear any response. However, prayers help you work out what you really need or want.

Meditation's what you need

Silent prayer allows people to focus on God. Meditation is also often silent, but it's not quite the same as prayer – it's not directed towards God, but inwards. Buddhists call it "mindfulness" as it focuses the mind on a particular thought in a calm and peaceful way. Buddhists meditate to develop positive attitudes and control negative ones.

WHAT goes on *in there?*

Wander into a church, temple, mosque, or synagogue and you'll witness all sorts of WORSHIP – ways to *honour God*. These may include prayers, rituals, meditation, offerings, ceremonies, and the study of holy books. Even the **architecture** and the **decor** of the building can have significance.

Inside a *CHURCH*

Music is used in many religions for inspiration, teaching, prayer, and meditation. Christian worship features different styles of music. Many cathedrals and monasteries still make use of plainsong – an unaccompanied singing style dating back to medieval times. Some churches feature choirs and organ music, and in many, the congregation sings hymns.

A picture is worth a *thousand words*

Orthodox churches contain icons – statues and paintings of holy people. Once, they taught the Bible to those who couldn't read. Today, they help people focus their prayers. Icons aren't worshipped, but respected for who they represent. People light candles near them, bow to them, or kiss them during prayer.

Inside a *MOSQUE*

There are three main elements to a mosque: a minaret (tower) at the top (the call to prayer is made from here); an entrance with fountains for ritual washing; and a main prayer hall with an alcove (*mihrab*) that indicates the direction of Mecca for prayer. There is also a pulpit from where sermons are given – but there are no chairs! People stand, bow, and kneel ritually as they pray.

Together but *apart*

Muslim men and women are instructed in the Qur'an to worship separately in order to prevent distraction. Often a mosque has separate rooms for men and women to pray in, though women usually stay at home to pray.

Inside a *SYNAGOGUE*

A Scroll of the Law (*Sefer Torah*) is the holiest object in Judaism. Scrolls are kept inside the holy ark in a synagogue, but are taken out, read from, and held up for everyone to see during prayer services. The ark and reading table (*bimah*), where the leader of the service stands, are the central focus of a synagogue. The congregation faces the ark – and Jerusalem – for prayers.

What did you say?

The language used in communal worship or prayer is not always the local language (the "vernacular"). For example, English synagogues have prayers in Hebrew, even though people speak English. Prayer books may have an English translation alongside the Hebrew to help people understand.

Inside a *GURDWARA*

Readings from holy scriptures are central to many worship services. During Sikh worship, verses from the *Guru Granth Sahib* (holy book) are chanted by a reader and repeated by the congregation in a song form called *shabad kirtan*. Any building that houses the *Guru Granth Sahib* is called a *Gurdwara*. The book is placed on a raised platform to honour God's presence in the teachings.

Let's go EAT!

After worship, Sikhs have a communal meal called a *langar*. *Karah parshad* – food that has been blessed – is given to all as a symbol of equality.

Home *SHRINES*

There are Hindu temples, but most regular worship takes place the home. *Puja,* a form of ritual worship in both temples and homes, may be addressed to any of the Hindu gods and goddesses through their icons and images (*murti*), which form the focus of home shrines. For many Hindus, the image represents the divine presence, but for some it is a manifestation of the presence.

JUST *DO IT!*

ICON OR IDOL?

Objects are often used in rituals, as a reminder of past events or as a focus of worship. Hindu worship is often centred on an icon (statue or picture of a god).

Ganesh, the Hindu elephant god

IDOL Some religions, though, object to anything that resembles idolatry (worship of false gods). The Ten Commandments, observed by Jews and Christians, state, "you shall not make for yourself any graven images".

Muslims believe that God cannot be represented in pictures: He is spirit, not physical. In Islam, images of God and even people are forbidden because they could mislead believers into worshipping the object rather than God. This is why Islamic buildings and books are decorated only with patterns and calligraphy (artistic writing).

Islamic tile

A RITUAL turns a person's

A RITUAL IS A SET PATTERN OF WORDS OR ACTIONS.

1 CLEANLINESS is next to *godliness*

Ritual washing is part of many religions. Evil is associated with dirt, while goodness and purity are linked to cleanliness. Muslims perform a hand-washing ritual called *wudhu* before prayer, since they must have a clean body and clothes for their prayers to be acceptable. Also, the act of cleansing encourages the right frame of mind for prayer.

Types *of*

2 *You are* what you EAT

Rituals are a key part of religious festivals. The *seder* meal at the start of the Jewish festival of Passover features food that symbolizes the story of how the Jews gained freedom from slavery in Egypt.

MATZAH (unleavened bread) is eaten at Passover, just as it was when the Jews fled Egypt – there was not enough time for their dough to rise.

A *seder* plate is used for the symbolic food.

A LAMB OR CHICKEN BONE represents the lamb sacrificed and eaten on the eve of the original Passover event – the exodus (leaving) of the Jews from Egypt. The bone is not eaten!

MAROR (bitter herbs) are eaten in memory of the bitter life of slavery in Egypt.

What's the first thing you do when you wake up? Some people say a blessing. Others wash their hands, or put their clothes on in a particular order. Religious life is full of such rituals – *but why?*

thoughts and beliefs into *actions*.

3 ACTING out *belief*

Many native religions involve belief in gods and ancestor spirits, who live in a different world. There are no teachings associated with this world – it's just accepted. People perform ritual dances or sacrifices to honour significant figures, acting out their beliefs instead of describing them.

RITUAL

4 Living *history*

Rituals often portray events in a religion's history, making them meaningful to people now. For Christians, Holy Communion, or the Eucharist, is a reminder of the last supper Jesus had with his disciples before he died.

The Bible account is read, and small portions of bread and wine are shared among the congregation. Roman Catholics believe that this bread and wine are transformed into the actual body and blood of Christ.

Holy Communion

5 ACTIONS speak *louder* than WORDS

Native North Americans use ritual to reflect their tradition. Dancing around a fire, totem pole, or drum symbolizes the belief that reality has a circular nature, with the One Great Spirit at its heart.

PROS AND CONS

Are rituals useful tools or meaningless distractions?

Find your focus

It can be hard to concentrate when praying, or to recall the historical event behind a festival, but rituals help keep things fresh and focussed. Performing them gets the whole body involved, not just the mind.

That's familiar

Rituals bring order and comfort: you always know what you should be doing. They also provide a sense of identity. Even in a foreign country where everything else is strange, you can usually find a familiar ritual.

Ritual rejection

Sikhs, Bahais, Quakers, and some other Christian groups are connected by their rejection of ritual.

Sikhs don't use ritual items such as statues or candles, as only God should be worshipped.

Bahais believe that rituals can become meaningless with repetition. They also think that, because rituals are always the same, they threaten individuality.

Quakers say rituals come between people and God. They meet in a plain room, where anyone may stand up and speak, or they pray in silence.

Festivals, FEASTS, and fasts

From *joyous* celebrations to days of fasting and contemplation, festivals mark important events in every religion's calendar.

VICTORY parade

The Sikh festival of *Hola* is held in memory of Guru Gobind Singh, a great warrior and military commander. During this one-day festival, Sikhs parade with colourful flags, carry out displays of martial arts, and take part in mock battles in the streets.

CELEBRATE!

Festivals can be **celebrations** of *special* events or people that have helped shape the religion.

Some *honour* religious figures...

Many founders of religions are commemorated on the *anniversary* of their birth or death (especially if their death was of religious significance). Religions with many gods often hold festivals to honour them at **different times** of the year.

... and some *celebrate* historical or seasonal events

There are festivals to celebrate every **occasion**: the **creation** of the world; *victory* in battle that ensured the survival of the religion; the time of the *first teachings* of the religion; spring festivals celebrating *new life*; autumn harvest festivals; winter festivals of light...

Lighting up life

The colourful festival of *Diwali*, or the Festival of Light, is an important time for Hindus, Sikhs, and Jains. It's a celebration of light against dark, good against evil, and knowledge against ignorance.

PARTY time

The Hindu festival of *Holi* heralds the new year and celebrates the spring harvest. Colourful powders are thrown about, pranks are played, and people dance in the streets. The usually strict Hindu social rules are relaxed and everyone gets covered in paint whatever their class, age, or gender.

Religious calendars

Almost every religion has its own calendar. Christianity follows the Gregorian calendar (the one we use in everyday life), and so the festival of Christmas always falls on the 25th December.

Some religions have a lunar calendar

where the months are based on the renewal of the moon. This calendar doesn't quite line up with the Gregorian one. For example, the Jewish new year always falls on the 1st of Tishri in the Hebrew calendar, which could be in September or October.

Contemplate...

Some holy days are special times of reflection, when people think over their actions and attempt to make up for any *wrongdoings*.

A time for repentance and *reflection*

In many religions, people are expected to **fast** (avoid eating) at special times of the year. Some fasts are a physical reminder of suffering, but others are a way of demonstrating *self-discipline* and restraint. By rejecting worldly distractions such as food, people can *concentrate* instead on more important things, such as developing their spirituality. Often the solemn festivals are followed by celebrations, showing that religion is not meant focus on the negative.

New *year*, new *you*

Rosh Hashana, the Jewish new year, is not a carefree party! Jews think about the deeds of the past year and ask for forgiveness from God in order to be inscribed in the book of life for another year. The book is sealed 10 days later on *Yom Kippur*, the Day of Atonement. Jews are encouraged to spend the entire day at the synagogue fasting and praying for forgiveness.

Sweet foods are eaten at *Rosh Hashana* to symbolize a sweet year to come.

Suffering *for others*

Muslims fast during the month of Ramadan in daylight hours to remind themselves of the suffering of the poor. The month ends with a celebration called *Eid-ul-Fitr*, when Muslims give thanks to God for the strength He has given them during their fast.

Remembering the resurrection

Easter is the most important time in the Christian calendar. It starts with Lent, a 40-day period of penance and prayer in which Christians remember Christ's suffering. Lent starts on Ash Wednesday and finishes on Good Friday, the day that Jesus was crucified. Easter Sunday is the celebration of his resurrection.

RITES OF PASSAGE

These religious ceremonies mark a change of status in life, from welcoming someone into the world or community to sending their soul onto a next life at death. *Weddings* and *funerals* are the most widespread rites of passage, but there are lots of others.

The sins a baby is born with are washed away at baptism.

Welcome to the world!

When a baby is born, he or she is not just a new addition to the family, but a new member of a religious community. Ceremonies that celebrate this include the Christian rite of baptism. This usually involves babies, but it may also be done for adults.

Joining the community

Children as young as seven can start a life of religious devotion. *Shinbyu* is when Theravada Buddhists become novice monks. Like the Buddha, the boys travel like princes to the monastery – then their heads are shaved to reject vanity.

Novice monks give up their finery.

What's in a name?

Sometimes, babies are called after religious leaders as a sign of respect, or in hopes that the baby will inherit good qualities. At a Sikh *Namakarana* naming ceremony, children are given a name based on a verse from scriptures.

Namakarana ceremonies take place in a *Gurdwara*.

Signing up for God

Aged eight days, Jewish boys are initiated in a circumcision ceremony called *brit milah*. This is when a boy is given both his name and his Jewish identity.

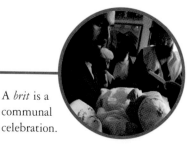

A *brit* is a communal celebration.

Purity and cleanliness

Muslim boys are circumcised too (called *khitan*). As well as being a sign of purity, *khitan* encourages cleanliness, which is essential for prayer.

Khitan usually takes place around the age of seven.

Rites of passage may be *celebrated* to HONOUR GOD, *obey religious laws,*

The sacred union

A colourful Hindu wedding reflects joy.

Weddings are joyous occasions, but they have a serious purpose. Marriage is not only a declaration of love – it's also a sacred union, possibly arranged by God. Marriage leads to children, and the religion passes to the next generation.

Burial allows a body to be resurrected.

The end of this life

Most religions don't see death as an end, but a passing to another life. Christians believe they will be reborn, so they may bury their dead so the body can be resurrected. Hindus cremate their dead, releasing the soul from this world into the next. Many scatter the ashes in the sacred River Ganges in India.

The River Ganges

COMING OF AGE   MARRIAGE   DEATH

The age of responsibility

Ceremonies such as confirmation (Christian) and *bar* and *bat mitzvah* (Jewish) celebrate adulthood – and the taking on of religious responsibilities. They usually happen in the early teens, when people are old enough to know right from wrong.

A girl is *bat mitzvah* at age 12.

In the presence of God

In almost every religion, weddings are performed by religious leaders. They involve making promises and receiving blessings in front of witnesses – including God.

Muslim wedding celebration

The Towers of Silence

Zoroastrians consider dead bodies to be impure. So instead of burial or cremation, they leave bodies on top of Towers of Silence to be destroyed by vultures, wind, or Sun.

The Towers of Silence in Iran

increase personal commitment, and make a **public declaration of faith.**

WHY do you wear *that?*

In hot countries, a *hijab* also provides protection from the Sun.

A *kippah* (skullcap) is worn to show respect for God.

A turban is not one of the Five K's, but is a sign of Sikh identity.

A *kirpan* represents courage, self-defence, and defence of the oppressed.

The *kara* is a physical reminder to live a moral life.

The *tzitzit* strings hang outside as a visible sign.

HIJAB...
FOR MODESTY

A Muslim woman is required to practise *hijab* (an obligation to cover the body) as an act of modesty so that she hides her beauty, saving it for her husband and close family. Some Muslims interpret this instruction to mean full coverage of the face and body (by wearing a *niqab*), while others understand it to mean coverage of the body and hair only.

A *niqab* acts as protection against unwanted attention.

TZITZIT...
AS A REMINDER

Jews are commanded to wear "*tzitzit* on the corners of their garments" to remind them of God's commandments. *Tzitzit* are knotted strings that were added to four-cornered garments commonly worn in biblical times. Today religious men wear a *tallit katan* under their shirt, which looks like a poncho with *tzitzit* on the corners.

A larger *tallit* is worn during morning prayers.

THE FIVE K'S...
FOR BELONGING

Members of the *Khalsa* (initiated Sikhs) wear all Five K's. Other Sikhs may wear some of these.
- *Kesh* (uncut hair) – symbol of God's will.
- *Kangha* (comb) – hair is combed twice a day to keep it clean.
- *Kachha* (under-trousers) – a symbol of self-restraint over desire.
- *Kirpan* – ceremonial sword
- *Kara* – steel bracelet

Women often wear headscarves instead of turbans.

Some followers of particular religions can be easily identified from the clothes they wear. The clothes and the reasons for wearing them may differ (and in many cases more than one reason applies), but all are an expression of belonging, which helps believers identify one another and form communities.

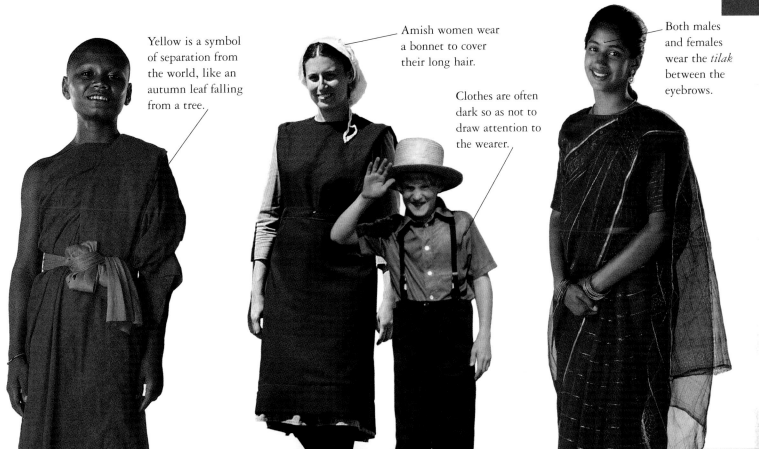

Yellow is a symbol of separation from the world, like an autumn leaf falling from a tree.

Amish women wear a bonnet to cover their long hair.

Clothes are often dark so as not to draw attention to the wearer.

Both males and females wear the *tilak* between the eyebrows.

ROBES...
FOR LETTING GO

Buddhist monks and nuns wear plain robes as a sign of a simple life, free of distraction. Different denominations traditionally wore different colours, largely based on what dyes were available in their area. Tibetan monks wear maroon, Zen Buddhists wear black, and Theravada monks and nuns wear orange or yellow.

PLAIN CLOTHES...
FOR HUMILITY

The Amish are strict Protestant Christians. Clothing laws are written into the *Ordnung* – rules of the Amish Churches. Clothes are plain symbols of humility – they have no decoration – no pockets, collars, or buttons. For the Amish, clothes are unimportant; fashion is a waste of time and money. What *is* important is living a good, modest life.

TILAK—
THE SACRED MARK

The *tilak* on a Hindu's forehead indicates where the spiritual eye opens. It's applied with sandal paste, sacred ashes, or *kumkum* (red tumeric), according to individual belief. Although the sari is closely associated with Hindu women, it has no religious significance – it's a traditional form of dress worn all over India.

Monks and nuns from all traditions wear robes.

Amish people don't wear belts, gloves, ties, or jumpers.

The *tilak* reminds Hindus of their religious daily goals.

HAIR *do's and don'ts*

You can make a real statement with *hair* – including a declaration of *religious* belief.

To cut...

> *Upanayana* is a "second birth" and is when I become an adult. I am given a sacred thread to wear, which I'll use during daily prayer rituals.

Sacred thread

As devotion
At the beginning of the coming of age ceremony known as *upanayana*, some Hindu boys have their head shaved by a *priest*, symbolizing the start of a new life of devotion to the gods.

For purification
At 1 or 2 years old, many **Hindu** babies have their first haircut in a ceremony called *mundan*. This practice is seen as a purification of child and a sacrifice of beauty, and parents pray for long life and riches for their child.

To reject the world
Buddhist monks shave their heads to copy the Buddha, who cut off his hair as a symbol of rejecting worldly things. The practice starts when young boys first leave home to become monks.

For submission
Male **Muslims** undertaking the pilgrimage to Mecca (the *Hajj*) shave their heads to declare themselves as slaves to God. Females also have a haircut (but it's not all shaved off!).

Not quite all
Followers of the **ISKCON** (*Hare Krishna*) movement shave their heads, but leave a tuft known as a *sikha*. This is said to protect the part of the brain linked with memories.

What people do with their hair can identify them as a follower of certain religions. For example, *Sikhs* won't cut their hair as it is a natural symbol of God's perfect creation. On the other hand (or head), some *Hindus* remove hair as a symbolic offering of service to their gods at special ceremonies.

... or not to cut

To be like Muhammad

Devout **Muslim** men grow their hair to look like Muhammad, keeping their beards long and trimming and combing them and their moustaches. Muslim women are expected to wear their hair long and kept covered when in public.

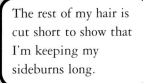

The rest of my hair is cut short to show that I'm keeping my sideburns long.

It's perfect as it is!

Sikh followers do not cut any of their hair, a practice known as *Kesh*. They comb their hair twice a day using a small comb called a *kanga*. Men tie their hair into a simple knot (or *joora*) and often cover this with a turban.

To avoid vanity

According to the **Amish** *Ordnung* rules, married men must let their beards grow but have no moustache, which is seen as vanity. Women can't cut their hair, but tie it back, hidden under a white cap or black bonnet.

Obeying God

Many Orthodox Jewish males let their sideburns grow long. This follows a rule in the *Torah* to not round off the corners of the head. This is also why many men have beards.

In fear of God

Followers of the **Rastafarian** movement can be recognised by their dreadlocks to symbolize a life in "dread" or fear of God. Dreadlocks are matted coils of uncut hair, which are washed only with pure water.

WHAT are *you* EATING?

Many religions (some more than others) have rules about diet, stating WHAT you can eat, what to *avoid* eating, and how to **prepare** the food. These laws are often based on sensible eating and food safety, but they also have religious symbolism.

Keeping *kosher*

Kashrut, the **Jewish dietary laws** set down in the Torah, are quite complicated. Acceptable foods are called kosher, from the Hebrew word for "fit" (see below). Totally non-kosher animals include pigs, shellfish, birds of prey, and insects. Products from these animals (such as gelatine) are also *treif* (non-kosher). All blood is *treif* too.

Kosher checklist

✓ Meat from animals with split hoofs and that chew the cud, such as cow and lamb.

✓ Meat from birds must be on the list given in the Torah, such as chicken and duck.

✓ Fish must have fins and scales, such as cod and trout — but not shellfish or rock salmon.

✓ Milk and other dairy products must come from kosher animals, such as cows and goats.

✓ Sweets, cakes, and other processed food can't contain products from non-kosher animals.

✓ Meat and dairy products must not be cooked or eaten together.

Dietary laws often come from scriptures, and may

Shellfish is out for Jews and Muslims

Fish is a sign of sacrifice for Catholics

Vegetarianism is common for Hindus and Jains

Kosher animals and birds must be slaughtered in a method called *shechita*, which is designed to cause minimum pain for the animal and to drain out as much blood as possible.

Drinking laws

The only dietary law of **Bahais** is no alcohol, a rule that is also observed by Muslims. Rastafarians won't drink alcohol, coffee, or milk.

also help preserve a sense of community within a religion.

...and bacon is not kosher or halal either

Digging up carrots may harm insects

Ital favours raw food where possible

VEGETARIAN non-violence

Many **Hindus** are vegetarian because they believe in the concept of *ahimsa* – "do no harm" – which includes not killing animals. Beef is not eaten at all: cows are sacred as a source of food and a symbol of life. But dairy products are seen as pure and are added to food. Devout **Jains** are vegan, even avoiding root vegetables as harvesting them may cause the death of insects. They also avoid blood-coloured foods such as tomatoes.

Halal and *haram*

Food allowed by **Islamic** law (set out in the Qur'an) is called *halal*. *Halal* animals, which are plant-eaters, cannot have died of natural causes. They have to be killed in a ritual way known as *zibah*, with minimum pain, while a dedication is recited. Forbidden *haram* foods include pork, birds of prey, meat-eating animals, and products from these animals.

FISH on Fridays

In the early days of **Christianity**, Wednesday and Friday fasts (marking Ash Wednesday and Good Friday), were common. These usually involved giving up meat, a luxury food that only the rich could afford. But anyone could catch fish from a lake, so fish was seen as the food of the poor. Today, giving up meat is still a sign of penitence (being sorry), and eating fish on Fridays is a common Catholic practice.

Ital: PURE food

Rastafarian dietary laws are called *ital*. Only natural food is *ital* – nothing processed, nothing tinned, and eaten raw as much as possible (which may be why many Rastafarians are vegetarian). *Ital* also includes some food laws from the Old Testament, such as no pork.

GIVE IT UP!

IMAGINE saying **goodbye** to your *family*, giving up your *home*,

THERE ARE *THREE* MAIN WAYS OF RENOUNCING

1 Seeking *SOLITUDE*

Solitude can be both mental (through meditation) and physical.

MEDITATION is part of many religions, disciplining the body so it can be ignored, and focus can centre on the spirit. Meditation can lead to greater wisdom, self-awareness, and insight.

PRAYERFUL SOLITUDE

Some Christian monks and nuns want to focus solely on prayer rather than leading an active life. They belong to "closed" or "cloistered" orders, and remain inside convents and monasteries.

2 Denying *PHYSICAL PLEASURES*

Some people feel that the body's physical demands hold them back from connecting with God, their inner self, or the inner truth. Their ways of resisting these demands include living a nomadic life; celibacy (no intimate relationships); and even giving up clothes!

Sannyasin

Sannyasa is the fourth stage of life in Hinduism. *Sannyasin*, or holy men, take vows of poverty and chastity, and wander around with few possessions, eating only when offered food. Dependent on God alone, they completely reject their lives and families. Some perform a funeral ceremony to show they are dead to the world.

A man must be over 50 (or a monk) to be a *Sannyasin*.

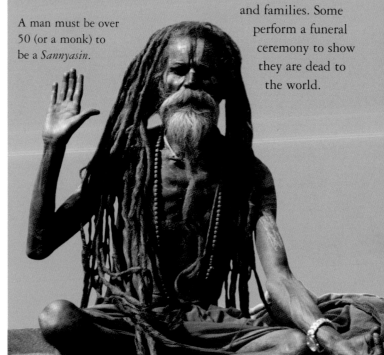

There are monks, nuns, and ascetics within many religions. These people publicly reject, or *renounce*, the world and instead practice asceticism. This self-denial and self-restraint **deepens their spiritual life** so they can get CLOSER to God and/or the true meaning of life.

going without *TV* or even *food...*

THE WORLD:

3 Seeking *DISCOMFORT*

For some people, acts of endurance, sleep deprivation, and even pain are part of the journey towards asceticism. During a religious vigil, they may go without sleep in order to pray or meditate. This may be done on the eve of a religious festival such as Easter, or at other times when they feel the need.

Giving it *ALL* up

Jain monks have five main vows of self-denial: celibacy, truth, no possessions, no stealing, and no violence. Male monks from one sect even reject clothes to show that they are beyond feelings such as modesty and shame.

OTHER VIEWS

Against asceticism

JUDAISM rejects asceticism on the basis that God wants creation to be enjoyed. The Talmud says that in the World to Come, people will have to account for every lawful pleasure they have given up.

SIKHS view self-denial as unhelpful for the development of the soul.

ZOROASTRIANISM does not allow self-denial, believing you should involve yourself in life through good words, deeds, and thoughts.

All things in *moderation*

Respecting asceticism

Buddhism, along with Jainism, values asceticism, and Buddhist lay people (non-ascetics) support their monks and nuns. However, the Buddha discouraged taking asceticism to an extreme. Buddhist monks follow the Middle Way – moderation in all things.

The ZEN way

Zen (a Japanese form of Buddhism) requires modified ascetic practices for short periods. These include celibacy, fasting after noon, and sleeping for short periods. These practices help to improve concentration during meditation.

A Zen circle is the Universe in one stroke.

> The physical world and the body are prisons of the soul.

Ascetic or *not*?

Early Christian monasticism was partly based on a theory from Plato, a Greek philosopher. Monasticism was later rejected by Protestantism.

Plato

The *search* for ANSWERS

WHAT ABOUT SCIENCE?

answers within...

What is GOD?

WHAT'S LIFE ABOUT?

This is the biggest question of all. It's also what religion is for: TO EXPLORE THE MEANING OF LIFE.

Philosophers have also asked questions about the meaning of life. Sometimes their answers support religious teaching, but sometimes they go against it. So,

What is God?
What about science?
What about morals?
Why is there so much bad stuff in the world?

Search for answers within...

Introducing philosophy

Philosophy (which means love of wisdom) has been an important part of most religions throughout history. It investigates the big questions such as

PHILOSOPHY IN RELIGION...

In the past, religious thinkers and teachers used philosophy to explore and explain their ideas. Philosophy wasn't a separate subject, and had less status than religious authority and revelation.

> "Philosophy is the handmaid of theology."

... AND PHILOSOPHY OF RELIGION

During the Enlightenment in the West, philosophy took on an authority of its own – people thought it should be "neutral", not coming from the viewpoint of a religion. Its aim was to test whether religious teachings, or even a whole religion, could be philosophically justified as being "true".

THOMAS AQUINAS *(1225–1274, Italy)*
Catholic priest and theologian who said that God has no form, He is perfect, infinite, and unchangeable, and His existence is part of His being.

People today disagree which is the best way.

A CLASSICAL PHILOSOPHICAL ARGUMENT

Much philosophy of religion, especially in the West, is concerned with debating God's existence. For example,

The divine watchmaker

1 *Of course there are stones in a desert. Not unexpected at all.*

Walking through a desert, you see two stones near each other.

2 *That's unusual. Someone must have been here and built that.*

You carry on walking and come across a wall of stones.

3 *Someone made that. Cogs and stuff wouldn't just arrange themselves into a watch by chance.*

Next, you find a watch lying on the ground.

# of religion

"What is God?" and "Why is there so much suffering in the world?"

West v East

WEST:

> What is God?

EAST:

> What is Goodness?

Philosophy covers lots of different ideas and means different things to different religions. For example, Western philosophy often deals with metaphysical* questions (especially questions about God) – things that Chinese philosophy is seldom concerned with at all. Eastern philosophy covers many viewpoints, including Chinese (Confucian and Taoist), Buddhist, Hindu, and Jain thought. Understanding the self and the concept of goodness are important ideas.

*Metaphysics means "beyond the physical". It's the part of philosophy that asks, "What is the nature of things? What is the world really about? Are we just a collection of atoms, or is there more to it?"

the design argument says that God must exist because the world, like a watch, is too complex not to have a designer or creator.

MEN OF SOUND MINDS

Throughout history there have been many religious thinkers and teachers who have made use of philosophy – a tradition that continues today.

SHANKARA *(8th century CE, India)* **Hindu ascetic and philosopher.** Used the *Veda* scriptures to conclude that there is no such thing as individuals, but that all souls are part of Brahman.

ABU HAMID AL-GHAZALI *(c.1055–1111, Iran)* **Sunni Muslim theologian and mystic.** Challenged the influence of Greek philosophy on Islam by saying that revelations in the scriptures don't need to be proven – they have higher authority.

MOSES MAIMONIDES "the Rambam" *(1138–1204, Spain and Egypt)* **Jewish rabbi, doctor, and philosopher.** His 14 books of *Mishneh Torah* (code to the Talmud) and *Guide to the Perplexed* are still used today to answer questions of Jewish law and ethics.

JOHN HICK *(born 1922, England)* **Perhaps the most influential modern philosopher of religion.** Promoted the idea of religious pluralism: no religion is more or less true than any other – all are paths towards to the goal of salvation.

4 EUREKA!
The world is far more complicated than a watch. It MUST have been designed, and that means it must have a designer. That designer is God.

5 *No, that can't be so!* *Well, that's how it is!*
Other philosophers disagree.

6 *But without a designer that would be like spilling ink on a page and expecting it to look like writing...*
The debate still continues today...

What's it all ABOUT?

What's the meaning of life? Why are we here?
Religion says that our purpose in life is to seek
the *ultimate truth* (which is sometimes called
the **ultimate reality**).

If you stripped away
the trappings of the
world to find out what lies
at **the heart** of existence,
what gives us a **purpose**,
what is *really REAL* in life
– **that** is the *ultimate
truth*. It could mean...

the
Supreme
Being
(God)

EXAMPLES OF ULTIMATE TRUTH

Buddhism says this
world is an illusion, full
of suffering. Ultimate
truth is escaping
from this through
enlightenment to
reach *nirvana*.

In **monotheistic**
religions, ultimate truth
is God. He is the Supreme
Being, giver of life and
creator of everything.
Salvation is to draw close
to Him, such as in heaven.

NOW I UNDERSTAND WHAT ULTIMATE TRUTH IS.

But what does *ultimate truth* MEAN?

the reason we're here

it can also be something that happens to us, a state of being such as enlightenment or salvation

the force that gives people life and soul

In **Hinduism**, ultimate truth is Brahman – a non-personal, cosmic principle. Salvation is to escape the cycle of rebirth and unite with Brahman.

On the other hand, **atheists** believe this world is all there is, and this is the ultimate truth.

ER… NOT QUITE. Human beings are the most intelligent animals on the planet, but even so, we have limited knowledge. We can only understand something by our own experiences, and describe something using language we know. But the ultimate truth is believed to be something far greater than language allows us to describe, something far more complicated than we can truly grasp. Religions present the ultimate truth in a way we can try to relate to, but they may only be part of a whole bigger picture.

WHAT *is* God?

We've mentioned God loads of times in this book. But *who* are we talking about, and WHAT is He (or She, or It) like?

AN OLD MAN WITH A BEARD?

People try to make the world easier to understand by giving things human qualities. We give names to machines and speak to our cars. And to make it easier to relate to God, some people think of Him as human-like too – maybe an old man with a beard (but far more powerful than actual humans).

BUT GOD ISN'T LIKE THAT.

God isn't a person. It isn't even a being. **God is the name religions give to the spiritual or supernatural reality that created and sustains the world.**

The LIMITS of language

God is unlimited – far greater than anything humans can truly understand or describe. But people can only relate to God using the words they have, which is a bit of a problem. Trying to describe God sets limits on what He's like or what He can do. Calling God "Father" doesn't mean He's our dad, but that He is caring, like a parent (but in a much greater way).

THE *NATURE* OF GOD

Monotheistic religions agree that God has particular attributes.

1 **ONENESS – there is one God**
However, "one" isn't just a number. It also means:

Unique –	**Eternal –**	**Self-existent –**
not one among many, but the only one, without equal.	always existed and will always exist. He has no beginning and no end.	God creates people, but no one created God.

OMNIPRESENT – always around God is everywhere, in every place at every time. God is both transcendent (beyond the world) and imminent (inside us).

OMNISCIENT – all-seeing and all-knowing God created the world, so He knows all about what's going on inside it. Many people believe that He knows how you will react to certain situations.

OMNIPOTENT – all-powerful
There is nothing that God cannot do.

WHOSE GOD IS HE ANYWAY?

Monotheists

These religions believe there is only one God in the world. Sikhs and Bahais believe that every religion shares the same God – different religions are just different ways of reaching Him.

Polytheists

Hinduism accepts many gods, but many Hindus believe there is one Supreme Power – Brahman – who is manifest (appears) in many ways, such as through the various gods.

Buddhist non-theism

God or gods are not part of most Buddhists' beliefs. However, some Mahayana Buddhists accept the existence of celestial (other-worldly) buddhas and bodhisattvas, who live in the heavens and may be honoured by believers to help them achieve enlightenment.

DOES GOD *EXIST?*

Philosophers have been arguing over this for centuries. The only conclusion is that it's not possible to prove His existence to people who don't believe. For believers, the reality of God is taken for granted.

What does God LOOK like?

NO ONE KNOWS. In the Bible, God tells Moses, 'You cannot see My face, for man shall not see Me and live". And the Qur'an says, "There is nothing like Him".

Is God MALE or FEMALE?

NEITHER. God has no body, so it's nonsense to ask if He is male or female. Calling God "He" is mostly convenience, but it can help people feel more connected than if He were called It.

Fred? ## What is God's NAME? Ethel?

MOSES ASKS GOD THIS VERY QUESTION in the Bible (Exodus 3:13). God replies, "I AM that I AM". (Also translated as "I will be what I will be".) This mysterious answer is taken by many to mean that He can't be defined – He can only be known by the actions He chooses to reveal to us.

So how do we KNOW about God?

THROUGH SCRIPTURES. Christians believe that God is reached through the word of Jesus Christ, His Son on Earth. Jews believe His will is revealed in the Torah, and for Muslims it is the Qur'an. The Sikh *Mool Mantar* prayer says that God is made known by the grace of the Guru.

GOD BY ANY OTHER NAME

Each of the theistic religions (those that believe in God) has different names and titles for God that describe His many characteristics. Here are just some.

Islam

Ar-Rahman – The All-Compassionate
Ar-Rahim – The All-Merciful
Al-Malik – The Absolute Ruler
Allah – the standard Arabic name for God. It is used by Muslims, and also by some small Christian and Jewish sects.

Christianity

Father
King (or King of Kings)
Judge
Jehovah
Almighty

Judaism

Adonai – my Lord
El Shaddai – God Almighty
Hashem – the Name, used in everyday speech. The Hebrew names of God can't be written in full (except in scriptures), because Jews are commanded not to destroy God's name.

Sikhism

Waheguru – Wonderful Teacher
Akal Purakh – Eternal One
Satnam – True Name/Eternal Reality
Ik Onkar – the One Creator

Zoroastrianism

Ahura Mazda – Wise Lord

Hinduism (names for Brahman)

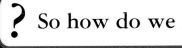

Ishvara – the Lord
Bhagavan – the Auspicious (successful) One
Parameshwara – the Supreme Lord

They can't ALL be

All religions claim to teach the truth about life's purpose, how people should behave, and what happens after we die. But there are many belief systems with different, even **contradictory teachings***. How can they all be true?

A recent *problem*

The worry of knowing whether you're following the right religion is just a few hundred years old. Early world religions started thousands of years ago in isolation from one another, so followers were not aware of different teachings in other parts of the world. Even today people's religion may be influenced by where they live – someone born in India is more likely to be a Hindu, but in America they are more likely to be Christian.

* For example, Christianity teaches God is incarnate (made real through Jesus); but in Islam this is blasphemy.

Ultimate
TRUTH!

WHO'S RIGHT?

There are three approaches to the problem that's known as *conflicting truth claims:*

Exclusivism

My religion is right and you won't achieve reality if you're not part of it or follow its rules. For example, some Christians believe that Jesus' words "I am the way, the truth, and life. No one comes to the Father but by me" mean that only Christianity offers salvation.

Inclusivism

My religion is right, but even if you're not part of it, you can find the truth too (though maybe in a limited way). Many strands of Hinduism, Sikhism, Buddhism, and Judaism are inclusive. Judaism says that Jews need to follow the Torah laws to reach the World to Come, but non-Jews can get there too if they follow a moral code.

Pluralism

Every form of religion is right, just different. The philosopher John Hick suggests the differences come from the influence of local culture and traditions, building a body around a backbone of religious teaching. The body looks different according to the culture that shapes it. Bahais believe that each religion reveals a different chapter of God's message to His people, and all religions lead to the same God.

FEELING THE ELEPHANT: a parable of pluralism

There is a parable in several Indian religions (Hinduism, Buddhism, and Jainism) that compares religion to six blind men wanting to find out what an elephant is like.

The first man felt its *side* and said an elephant was like a WALL.

The second felt its *tusk* and said an elephant was like a SPEAR.

The third felt its *trunk* and said an elephant was like a SNAKE.

right! (Can they?)

TRUTH!

CLIMBING *mountains*

John Hick compared religious pluralism to climbing a mountain – there are many paths up the mountain but they all lead to the same summit: **ultimate truth.** The paths and summit might look different (in Buddhism it's *nirvana*; in Christianity it's salvation with God in heaven), but that's only because it appears in ways that are understood by each person.

There are many

Hinduism · Baha'i · Confucianism · Judaism · Islam · Christianity · Buddhism · Sikhism

religious routes to the top.

HOWEVER...

Not everyone agrees that religions all lead to the same ultimate truth.

ONLY my road *exists*

There are some people within many of the main world religions who believe theirs is the true and exclusive religion.

MANY roads, many *destinations?*

Theologian John Bowker points out that words can't describe the "ultimate truth", so this term may mean something different in each religion – in the same way as not all roads lead to New York, even though they are all roads.

The *jury* is OUT...

Some people believe their own religion to be true, but are "agnostic" about others – they won't judge whether others may be true or not because only God (or other ultimate truth) can know.

The fourth felt its *leg* and said an elephant was like a TREE.

The fifth felt its *ear* and said an elephant was like a FAN.

The sixth felt its *tail* and said an elephant was like a ROPE.

The *moral* of the STORY

is that each man could only report what he had felt and understood. He wasn't wrong, but didn't know the full picture. It's the same with the ultimate truth – we may not know the whole truth. When other religions appear to say something different, they may just be describing a different part of it.

If religions preach PEACE,

Every religion has a version of the golden rule:

Love your neighbour as yourself.

JUDAISM: "What is hateful to you, do not do to your neighbour: that is the whole Torah; the rest is commentary." *Rabbi Hillel, Talmud, Shabbat 31a*

SIKHISM: "I am a stranger to no one; and no one is a stranger to me. Indeed, I am a friend to all." *Guru Arjan Dev, Guru Granth Sahib 1299*

BUDDHISM: "Treat not others in ways that you yourself would find hurtful." *Udana-Varga 5:18*

HINDUISM: "This is the sum of *dharma* (duty): do not do to others what would cause pain if done to you." *Mahabharata 5:1517*

ISLAM: "None of you truly believes until he desires for his brother that which he desires for himself." *Muhammad, recorded in the Hadith*

CHRISTIANITY: "So in everything, do to others what you would have them do to you, for this sums up the Law and the Prophets." *Jesus, New Testament Gospel of Matthew 7:12*

The golden rule should be followed by everyone and include everyone: children and adults, males and females, people of the same faith, other faiths, or none at all.

It demonstrates two things: that you should care about all people, not just those of your own religion; and that religion is concerned with society as well as individuals – you cannot be good to yourself (and so find salvation or enlightenment) without being good to other people.

We're all here to help each other.

Care in the community

People within a community often help each other. Many religions have laws for giving to charity. The point of charity is not to earn points for yourself, but to help those who cannot support themselves. As well as giving money or food, communities may set up schools, hospitals, or other groups.

"There will be peace on EARTH when there is peace

WHY is everyone *fighting?*

US + THEM = INTOLERANCE

Religious intolerance comes from two sources: non-believers who target all religion; and religious people who disagree with other religions. Both are rooted in people's tendency to see the world in terms of "us and them":

> **US = people like me**
> (*such as my family, class, religious group, age, or race*)
>
> **THEM = people who aren't like me**

When people are different, they're an easy target for hatred. Those with a different way of life are persecuted because society doesn't understand them. Ignorance leads to fear, and fear leads to intolerance. Sometimes, this causes governments to ban religious practices, and believers to become defensive.

"Why are you doing that? It's stupid."

Fundamentalism...

Almost every religion has fundamentalists – people who believe their religion is the only way to live and reach salvation. Some believe that others should follow their path to salvation too, so they become missionaries or organize political protests to spread their teachings.

... and extremism

A small percentage of fundamentalists are extremists. They use violence and terror to draw attention to their religion. They may justify their actions by saying they're following God's will – but they ignore their scriptures' instructions to respect human life.

What about the golden rule?

Some people say that respecting different beliefs is not the same as tolerating them. Missionaries respect non-believers, but still want to change their views. Violent extremists would probably only apply the golden rule to people who are *exactly* like them – if at all.

among the WORLD RELIGIONS." Hans Kung, theologian

WHY do *bad things*

When a murderer kills innocent people, some may wonder why God

WHY IS THERE SUFFERING?

The "problem of evil" is a classic argument in western philosophy. It says:

1 God is all-powerful
2 God is all-good
3 There is evil present in the world

The conclusion is that either God is not all-powerful and can't stop evil; or He is not all-good and doesn't want to.

Some religious *responses*

People have free will and you can't blame God for their actions if they choose to do evil to others.

Suffering is necessary in order for people to develop spiritually and draw closer to God.

Suffering can lead people to do acts of kindness for each other.

Suffering is a test of faith. Those who pass will be rewarded – now or in the next life.

Suffering is a punishment for wrongdoing.

A WESTERN view
How can God let people suffer?

FREE WILL

The main explanation for bad things happening in the world is that people have made them happen. Monotheistic religions say that God created a perfect world, but also gave people FREE WILL – freedom to choose to do good or bad things. Bad choices have made the world imperfect.

Why didn't God create people **to do only good?**

Because then, it could be argued, we are not truly free: we won't have been created with the ability to choose our actions. With free will, some people choose to do the wrong things, making others – or themselves – suffer.

Is it worth it?

Some people say that suffering is necessary in order for better things to happen. Free will may bring suffering, but without it we could not grow spiritually (in the likeness of God). What we can gain far outweighs what we can lose.

Job's story

Mostly scriptures say it's not for us to know why bad things happen – only God knows. The Bible puts it this way:

Job was in the centre of an argument between God and the Devil.

The Devil tries his hardest...

Job is such a good man. He always does as he's told.

Satan, you are so wrong. Job could suffer and he would still obey Me.

Job's camels are stolen.

His servants are killed by enemies.

Sheep die.

He gets ill.

His children die when his house is destroyed.

RUBBISH! He only obeys you to get your blessings.

We'll see...

happen to *good people?*

didn't stop it. Others may ask if they **did something** to *deserve* it.

An EASTERN view

What are people doing wrong?

KARMA

In polytheistic and non-theistic Eastern religions, people don't ask "How can God let us suffer?" Instead, Hinduism and Buddhism teach that suffering is the result of *karma*. This means that good deeds will produce good outcomes, while bad actions lead to bad fortune, in both this and future lives.

What is wrongdoing?

HINDU teachings

The *Bhagavad Gita* scripture says that people "should know properly what action is, what forbidden action is, and what inaction is." The wrong action leads to bad *karma*, which causes suffering in this life or a future one. The suffering may affect the individual, or a group of people.

The BUDDHIST view

The Buddha taught that *dukkha* (suffering) comes from people not seeing the world as it truly is – empty. Instead, people form attachments to the world, which stop them reaching enlightenment. However, **awareness** of suffering is the start of the journey towards **freedom** from it.

SO WHAT'S THE ANSWER?

It depends on *which* religion you ask!

The purpose of suffering is related to a religion's teaching of the purpose of life. Some say suffering is necessary to grow spiritually, but others think it's a problem to be overcome by reaching enlightenment.

However, everyone agrees: *we want suffering to end.*

This means showing compassion to others, easing their suffering on Earth.

The *end* of suffering

Religions differ on what this means. For some the end of suffering will happen on Earth; for others, in an afterlife. Some say it's enlightenment; for others it's the arrival of a messiah (or messianic age) to bring peace into the world.

Mrs Job finally has enough.

Just curse God so you will die and escape this misery.

Are you mad? What makes you think that will bring good? I won't curse God.

Eventually, Job complains to his friends.

It's not fair! What have I done to deserve this?

You must have sinned to be punished like this.

God responds…

I made the world and only I know why things happen. When you have My experiences and can create the world, then you can ask. It's not your place to know.

God rewards Job with health, wealth, and more children for putting up with it all.

Religion and *science*

In the past, religion had answers for everything. *How old is Earth? How did it get here? How did we humans get here?*

WHAT HAPPENS WHEN RELIGION

CONFLICT

Some people think science is a direct threat to religion because it attempts to disprove religious beliefs. The best-known debate is between Darwin's theory of evolution and creationism. It started in Britain in the 1860s, and only lasted a couple of decades before the fuss died down, but it's been revived recently by atheists such as biologist Richard Dawkins, and remains alive in some parts of the USA.

"You cannot be both sane and well educated and disbelieve in evolution. The evidence is so strong that any sane, educated person has got to believe in evolution."

Richard Dawkins *(1941–)*

CO-OPERATION

This is the view that science and religion can use each other's discoveries to further their own ideas. Some scientific theories may appear to challenge religion, but they actually share common ground. After all, science hasn't yet found all the answers.

I think life started with a burst of light.

"Scientists have discovered that the Universe began with the vast, sudden, and inexplicable explosion of light popularly known as the big bang. This could be the scientific version of the Scriptures' God said, "Let there be light, and there was light.""

Physicist **Nathan Aviezer**

*Of course science had always existed, but mostly sat happily alongside religious beliefs. For example, Aztecs and ancient Egyptians used astronomy to work out where to build their temples, and when to perform particular ceremonies.

Then SCIENCE came along (especially since the Enlightenment*). Suddenly there were new answers. New people had authority – scientists rather than priests. New ideas had to be tested and proven. People were no longer happy to accept the word of scripture: they wanted evidence. So what did this mean for religion?

MEETS SCIENCE?

NOTHING AT ALL!

The majority view, and the one that killed off the original evolution/religion challenge, is that science and religion deal with different things, so there is no conflict. Even Darwin didn't see a clash between evolution and belief in God, and today there are many scientists who are also religious.

LABORATORY

"Objective knowledge [ie science] provides us with powerful instruments for the achievements of certain ends, but the ultimate goal itself and the longing to reach it must come from another source."

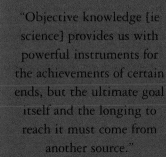

Albert Einstein *(1879–1955)*

WHAT IS CREATIONISM?

Every religion has its account of how the world began. The biblical story of creation, part of Judaism and Christianity, tells how God made the world and everything in it in six days – but it's understood in different ways.

Some people take it literally. If the Bible says that's what God did, then that's how it is. Maybe God created fossils and buried them during the creation. They may appear millions of years old, but how do we know we've dated them accurately?

Some see it as symbolic. The creation story isn't meant to be taken literally – it teaches that God created the world. Perhaps the "days" of creation weren't 24 hours, but six periods of time that lasted thousands or millions of years. This is when humans evolved under God's management.

Others don't accept it at all but say that Earth formed out of nowhere in the "big bang", and humans evolved rather than being created by God.

Where *did* Earth come from?

Many scholars in different religions have also been doctors. And the Islamic concept of *Tawhid* (God's Oneness) teaches that all things are part of God, including understanding the world through science.

THE MORAL MAZE

WHAT IS *MORALITY*?

Morals are standards of acceptable behaviour – in other words, knowing what's good and what's bad. Some people think you can't be moral if you aren't religious (because religion gives people a moral code to follow). Others think it's perfectly possible to be moral without any kind of religious belief.

So how *DO* people make **MORAL** **DECISIONS**?

> I use my instinct to know what's right or wrong.

> I refer to holy books and sacred texts.

Reaching an ANSWER may involve **more** than *one* decision

> I make my decision on compassionate grounds.

> I try to copy the lives and actions of holy men.

> I use reason to find a logical outcome.

> I look for the karmic outcome of the decision.

When people behave **WELL**, everybody is *happier*, and

Each religion has moral laws that GUIDE its believers – but the right way to live *differs* between religions and even groups **within** a particular religion. Some moral laws, such as the **golden rule** (see page 80), occur in many belief systems, but others are *unique* to one.

> I abide by ancient religious customs.

MORAL *DILEMMAS*

Most of us have a set moral code to help us make decisions, but life is sometimes too complicated for rules, and we have to make tricky choices.

 The Ten Commandments state, "Thou shalt not steal". What if Christians or Jews are lost in the country, and their children are hungry? Would they take food from a farmer's field?

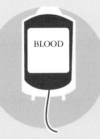 Jehovah's Witnesses don't believe in blood transfusions. Say Witnesses have a teenage son who disagrees – if he were going to die without blood, would they agree to it?

The Qur'an teaches that lying is a sin. Would a devout Muslim tell an otherwise harmless lie to avoid hurting another person?

> I look to the teachings of religious leaders.

 Hindus are forbidden from doing harm to any life. But what if they had to kill a wild beast to save a child?

THIS *way* please

Where do people of different religions find their moral codes and advice?

JUDAISM – Jews abide by 613 commandments set down by learned and respected elders and rabbis. They also follow Jewish custom.

ISLAM – Muslims lead a moral life by following the Qur'an, Sunnah (the examples of Muhammad), and *shari'a* (Islamic law, seen as divine authority).

CHRISTIANITY – Christians use the teachings and examples of Jesus, as set out in the Bible, as a model for their own actions. Church tradition is important too.

BUDDHISM – To lead moral lives, and break free from the cycle of suffering, Buddhists must adhere to the Five Precepts and follow the steps of the Noble Eightfold Path.

SIKHISM – Sikhs address questions of what is right and what is wrong by referring to the Sikh holy book, the *Guru Granth Sahib*.

HINDUISM – Hindus follow their *dharma* according to their stage and status in life, and receive guidance from the 10 *yamas* and 10 *niyamas* of ancient scripture.

society is healthier and more *prosperous*.

IS religion

YES! RELIGION has *served its purpose.* It's time to MOVE ON.

Some scholars who study human behaviour believe that people invented religion and gods. Belief in gods was a necessary and important stage of human development, when people needed them for protection or to explain why things happened. But now we've outgrown this belief. Humanity can stand on its own two feet, we don't need gods to protect us. We can turn to science for answers and our actions are guided by well-informed and rational thoughts.

> We don't NEED God to tell us how to behave. People **naturally** know what's right and wrong. And if they forget, well, we have *state laws*.

> *Modern science tells us* **EVERYTHING** *we need to know about the world – and* disproves *the stuff in the scriptures.*

> I just DON'T think there's any such thing as God.

redundant?

NO! RELIGION is *alive and well.*

For believers, religion teaches higher truths. We still need religion to answer important questions, ones that not even science can answer. It provides a connection to the past, and can offer people a sense of belonging and purpose. Though religion may be on the decline in Western Europe, elsewhere it is still going strong, even growing. More than three-quarters of the people in the world say they have some sort of religious belief.

My religion is my **WAY OF LIFE.** I like doing the things that my people have been doing for centuries – it gives me a **PURPOSE** and a sense of **BELONGING.**

My religion is TRUE and it remains true, even if it becomes *unfashionable.*

Science tells us about our physical *world, but it is **NOT ABLE** to tell us about the* non-physical *world, or about metaphysical truths and meanings.*

Who's *who?*

All religions have had special teachers or leaders who spread its teachings and helped people understand them. Most of what we know about these figures comes from oral (spoken) tradition that was later written down, and from holy books.

ABRAHAM
JUDAISM, ISLAM, CHRISTIANITY

ZARATHUSTRA (ZOROASTER)
ZOROASTRIANISM

MOSES
JUDAISM, ISLAM, CHRISTIANITY

LAOZI (LAO-TZU)
TAOISM

According to Hebrew scriptures, Abraham – at a time of idol worship – believed in one God, Who promised that he would be the father of a great nation. Abraham had two sons: Isaac, by his wife, and Ishmael, by his servant. Abraham, Isaac, and Isaac's son Jacob are the fathers of Judaism. For Christians, they are Jesus' ancestors, and in Islam, Ishmael is the ancestor of Muhammad.

Zarathustra, a priest, lived in part of Asia that is now Iran and Afghanistan. His meditations on good and evil led to a divine revelation about two spirits in constant battle, one good and one evil – the world and mankind were created by God, the good spirit, to help in this battle. His views first became popular in Bactria (Afghanistan), then spread to nearby kingdoms.

Hebrew scriptures describe Moses as a prophet and a lawgiver. Born a Hebrew, he was adopted and raised as a Egyptian prince. God made him leader of the Hebrews and he led them out of slavery in Egypt into the promised land of Canaan (now Israel). Through Moses, God gave the people a set of laws, which are recorded in the Jewish Torah and the Christian Bible.

Tradition suggests that Laozi was a philosopher in ancient China, and a court scribe. The Tao text attributed to him, *Te Ching*, together with a text by Zhuangzi, is seen as the central authority of Taoism. There are, however, some historians who think Laozi may be a mythical person, or a combination of several different historical figures.

"The way is not in the **sky**. The way is in the *heart*."

"To know your **faults** and be able to *change* is the greatest virtue."

"Love your neighbour as yourself."

BUDDHA (SIDDHARTHA GAUTAMA) 6TH–5TH CENTURY BCE BUDDHISM	MAHAVIRA 6TH CENTURY BCE JAINISM	CONFUCIUS (K'UNG-FU-TZU) 551–479 BCE CONFUCIANISM	JESUS C. 5 BCE–30 CE CHRISTIANITY, ISLAM

Born a prince, Siddhartha Gautama suddenly became aware of human suffering during a trip outside his palace. He was determined to find a way for people to make their lives better. He finally achieved *nirvana* (blissful enlightenment) while meditating under a fig tree, when he became known as the Buddha (and the tree became the Bodhi tree). He spent the rest of his life teaching people how to find enlightenment.

Mahavira is the 24th Jina ("teacher that shows the way") of Jainism. Born Prince Vardhamana in India, he gave up his life of luxury when he was 30 to become an ascetic. After 12 years of fasting and meditation, he achieved enlightenment and became known as Mahavira ("great hero"). Afterwards, he taught this enlightenment to others.

Confucius was born in China. A great thinker, he also had a strong belief in education for all, and his ideas attracted many disciples (followers). He claimed that self-discipline and compassion for others were not new ideas, but were in ancient Chinese philosophy. Confucius' teachings and conversations are recorded in the *Lunyu* (*Analects*), written around the 2nd century BCE.

Born Jewish, Jesus is seen as a prophet in Islam and as God's Son by Christians. A preacher, healer, and teacher, he had many followers during his three-year ministry in Galilee (Israel), who believed he was the Messiah (saviour) promised by their ancestors. Seen as a dangerous rebel, he was killed by the Romans, but followers believe he rose three days later, before ascending into heaven.

Who's who *too?*

NAGARJUNA	MUHAMMAD	ABU BAKR	'ALI
C. 100–165 CE	C. 570–632 CE	CALIPH REIGN:	CALIPH REIGN:
BUDDHISM	ISLAM	632–634 CE	656–661 CE
		SUNNI MUSLIM – ISLAM	SHIA MUSLIM – ISLAM

According to tradition, Nagarjuna was a Hindu who converted to Buddhism. Seen widely as an influential Indian philosopher, he is called the second Buddha by Tibetan and East Asian Buddhists, and his writings are the basis of the Madhyamaka (Middle Way) school of Buddhism. Nagarjuna proposed that the true nature of all things is emptiness; all things are without essence, and only exist in relation to other things.

Muhammad had his first revelations from God while meditating, and three years later began revealing them publicly. After a hostile reception, he retreated to Yathrib (Medina, Saudi Arabia), but later returned to conquer Mecca. Muhammad's divine revelations form the Qur'an. Muslims believe that neither God nor people should ever be portrayed, which is why faces are veiled in Islamic art.

Abu Bakr, Muhammad's father-in-law, was one of his a close companions. When Muhammad died, Abu Bakr was elected leader, or caliph, of Muhammad's Islamic state. He led military campaigns against rebel communities, and within two years he had united Arabia into a single, Muslim-controlled state.

Shia Muslims regard 'Ali, the son-in-law and cousin of Muhammad, as the first imam (religious leader), and his descendents as the successors to Muhammad. 'Ali was close to Muhammad during his time in Yathrib, and eventually, Ali was appointed his successor.

Mecca →

"Forgiveness is God's command."

"The word is the Guru now."

GURU NANAK	MARTIN LUTHER	GURU GOBIND SINGH	BAHA'U'LLAH
1469–1539	1483–1546	1666–1708	(MIRZA HUSAYN
SIKHISM	CHRISTIANITY	SIKHISM	'ALI NURI)
	(PROTESTANTISM)		1817–1892

Nanak was born Hindu, and studied Hinduism and Islam intensively. Later, he became convinced by a vision that there is only one God, before whom all people are equal. Nanak spent his life debating with holy men, and teaching his belief that people's soul, and the way they behave, is more important than rituals or pilgrimages. He wrote his thoughts down as poetry, and his poems are still sung as hymns by Sikhs today.

Originally a Catholic monk and theologian, Martin Luther became concerned with indulgences (money paid to priests for spiritual advantage) and other abuses of power, and eventually questioned his faith. He published his opinions in his *95 Theses* (1517), and was excommunicated in 1521. Luther continued to promote his ideas and to reform churches, eventually becoming the founder of Protestantism.

Born in 1666, Gobind Singh became the 10th and last guru on the death of his father Guru Tegh Bahadur. In 1699, his view that no power could exploit the Sikhs led him to create the *Khalsa Panth*, a body of "soldier saints" who wore special identity symbols. Before he died, he announced that there would be one final and eternal Guru – the Sikh scriptures, called the *Guru Granth Sahib*.

Founder of the Bahai faith, Baha'u'llah was born Muslim in Persia (Iran), but later became a follower of the Bab, a prophet who claimed there would be another prophet after Muhammad. After the Bab's death, he was imprisoned and later exiled. A divine vision encouraged him to record his thoughts and revelations, which now form the Bahai scripture. He is seen by believers as God's prophet.

GLOSSARY

Key
(B) Buddhism
(C) Christianity
(Co) Confucianism
(H) Hinduism
(I) Islam
(Ja) Jainism
(J) Judaism
(S) Sikhism
(T) Taoism

afterlife Life after death.

alms Offering money or food to the poor.

ascetic A person who practises extreme self-discipline.

atman (H) Human soul.

atonement (C, J) Becoming reconciled ("at one") with God.

baptism (C) A rite in which water is used to symbolize someone's admittance into the Church.

bar mitzvah (J) The coming-of-age ceremony for 13-year-old boys.

bat mitzvah (J) The coming-of-age ceremony for 12-year-old girls.

Bible (C) A collection of religious writings divided into the Old and New Testaments.

Brahma (H) The first god of the Hindu Trimurti, Creator of all things.

Brahman (H) The Supreme Power, who is inside all things.

Buddha (B) Someone who has achieved enlightenment and teaches others to do the same; the Buddha was Siddhartha Gautama.

caliph (I) Historically, a leader of Islam.

celibacy Giving up intimate relationships.

church (C) A body of believers; a building for worship.

congregation A group of people gathered together for worship.

convent (C) A community, especially of women (nuns), living under religious vows.

covenant Agreement.

crucifixion (C) A method of execution by tying or nailing someone to a wooden cross. Jesus was crucified.

deity A god or goddess.

denomination a branch (group) within a religion.

dharma (B) The teaching of the Buddha. (H) The law of existence, right conduct.

disciple Someone who follows another person's teachings.

divine Of God or a god.

doctrine A body of religious teachings.

Enlightenment, The An 18th-century movement that stressed the importance of science and reason.

enlightenment (B, H) The state of spiritual knowledge that frees people from the cycle of dying and being reborn.

faith A strong belief in the doctrines of a religion.

Gurdwara (S) A place of worship, where the *Guru Granth Sahib* is installed.

Guru Granth Sahib (S) The holy Sikh scriptures and spiritual guide.

Hadith (I) A account of something said or done by Muhammad.

hajj (I) Pilgrimage to Mecca.

halal (I) Lawful according to Islamic law. Often used in relation to food.

Hebrew Bible (J) *See* Tanakh.

Holy Communion (C) A ceremony where bread and wine, representing Christ's body and blood, are shared. Also called the Eucharist.

icon (C) A statue or picture of a holy figure, used to aid worship.

idolatry Worship of false gods.

imam (I) Leader of ritual prayer in the mosque; leader of an Islamic school of thought; for Shias, messengers of divine light with exceptional spiritual authority.

kami Powers of nature in the Shinto religion.

karma (B, H) People's actions, good or bad, that determine their future existence once they die and are reborn.

Khalsa (S) The group that initiated Sikhs belong to.

khanda (S) One of the most important Sikh symbols.

kosher (J) Fit for use according to Jewish law, especially used of food.

mantra (B, H) A repeated word or sound used to aid meditation.

meditation To focus deeply on something for a period of time as an aid to spirituality.

messiah (C, J) Promised saviour. In Judaism, the messiah is foretold by the ancient prophets. In Christianity, the Messiah is Jesus Christ.

moksha (B, H, Ja) State of release from the cycle of birth and death. Also known as *mukti*.

monastery A community of men living under religious vows.

morality A code of conduct that distinguishes between good and bad behaviour.

mosque (I) A place of worship.

nirvana (B, H) Liberation; freedom from suffering, desire, and sense of self.

observance The practise of following a particular law or ritual.

orthodox Following what is considered to be the established, traditional view.

pagan Someone who holds religious views that differ from those of the main world faiths; often used now of nature-worshipping traditions.

penance An act of repentance (feeling sorry) for wrongdoing.

philosophy Study of the nature of knowledge and existence.

priest Someone authorized to carry out religious ceremonies.

prophecy Divine prediction.

prophet Teacher, or messenger of God.

puja (B, H) Worship.

Qur'an (I) The holy book of Islam, believed to contain the holy words of God as revealed to Muhammad.

rabbi (J) Teacher or leader.

redeemer (C) Someone who saves others from sin, to make up for their wrong behaviour.

Reformation (C) The process of breaking away from the Roman Catholic Church that gave rise to Protestant Christianity.

reincarnation (B, H, Ja) The cycle of dying and being reborn, to which all life in this world is subject.

Resurrection (C) Jesus' rising from the dead, in which all Christians will participate.

revelation A religious truth revealed in an extraordinary way.

rite A religious ceremony or act.

ritual A ceremony that consists of a series of actions, words, and movements carried out in a specific order.

Sabbath (C, J) A holy day of rest.

sacrament (C) A religious ceremony that is regarded as an outward sign of an inner blessing or grace.

sacrifice An offering made as an act of thanksgiving or atonement.

salat (I) Prayer, performed in a set way five times a day.

salvation (C) The act of being saved from the effects of sin by faith in Jesus.

samsara (B, H) See reincarnation.

sannyasi (H) A holy man who relies solely on alms, and is in the last of the Hindu four stages of life.

scriptures Holy writings.

secular Not governed by religious rules.

shabad kirtan (S) A form of musical chanting that has a call followed by a response.

shaman A priest of indigenous (native) religions believed to possess higher powers.

shari'a (I) Islamic code of law.

shrine A holy place associated with a god or sacred person.

soul The essential inner nature of someone's spiritual self.

swami (H) A holy man or member of a religious community.

synagogue (J) A place of worship and study.

Talmud (J) Record of rabbis' interpretations of Jewish scriptures.

Tanakh (J) The Hebrew scriptures, containing the Torah. Also called the Hebrew Bible.

temple A building used for worship.

theology Religious beliefs and the theory behind them.

Torah (J) God's law, revealed to Moses.

Trimurti (H) The three main Hindu Gods: Brahma, Vishnu, and Shiva.

Trinity (C) One God in three parts: Father, Son, and Holy Spirit.

Vedas (H) Ancient Hindu scriptures in four main parts or collections.

yang (Co, T) One half of the Chinese concept of nature and the Universe, associated with creativity, masculinity, heaven, heat, and light.

yin (Co, T) One half of the Chinese concept of nature and the Universe, associated with femininity, Earth, dark, and cold.

yoga (B, H) Discipline involving mental, physical, and spiritual exercise.

yogi (H) A person who is skilled in yoga.